A LOGICAL GUIDE TO SEEING AND UNDERSTANDING CORRUPT POLITICIANS
The NEW American Revolution: Reclaiming Our Government from the Crooks Who Hold it Hostage

By- Dante Kali Das

A LOGICAL GUIDE TO SEEING AND UNDERSTANDING CORRUPT POLITICIANS: The NEW American Revolution: Reclaiming Our Government from the Crooks Who Hold it Hostage

Copyright 2012 Dante Kali Das

ISBN: 978-3-0003582-3-4

Published by: Kali Das Publishing

Other titles by Dante Kali Das: "Don't Tread On Me 2012: The Elite Deadline and the Coming World Economy Crash"

DEDICATION AND THANK YOU

For my family who has endured all and stayed through it all.
In loving memory of Dipsy and Meera who were killed by these agents.

Special thanks to Monica for helping me with technical issues involving the printing of this book. Thanks to Erik as well.

.

And as always for Mother Meera and Babaji. Thank you Mother Meera.

For all within Stalking, Mobbing, Street Theater, and for all dealing with this Technology. This is for you (And if not for this Technology this book would be in better shape).

Also for Kylie in the hope that she one day wakes up and knows the Truth.

For all people doing their part and speaking out for change, for all those on the Path of Consciousness.
Also for those within government, agencies, and law enforcement who are not corrupt and doing their part.

Special thanks to Sasha and the song, "Hide and Seek" which is about "The Three Investigators", this is my song.

S.R.D.
TABLE OF CONTENTS

INTRODUCTION

"Any American who turns a blind eye to injustice and corruption around him should not be allowed to call himself one- it is by definition fighting these things that makes us an American in the first place. In being an American we carry this responsibility." - Mr. Lee

This is a book for everyone these days, and to some extent it is a collection of essays, but not exactly. As my last book was I find I am in a rush here to get this done while having technical difficulties due to "others". Read on to get a better idea.

This is a book about corruption and corrupt people. It is a guide to seeing corrupt people and their plans which are all around us. This is to some extent the story of my life as well- corruption has destroyed my life and now destroys my family's, which I will get to. It is my intent to point out by example and logic, to explain the mentality and psychology of the corrupt rich and powerful amongst government and industry, those who I call the Elite. It is my intent to explain this type of person, to make them more easy to understand and therefore easier to see as too few people actually get or understand this type of person, therefore they remain invisible to the public. It is also my intent to point out various plans they have picked out for the world and how we can see these plans- the pieces of the puzzle which point to this. I take from the media what looks like various individual pieces and like a detective I show how they all fit together as part of a bigger plan and bigger picture. My understanding of these people coming from and being based on my life.

I will start all of this by getting into my life, both the past and present, and then I will apply this to what I see happening in our world today. Consider this introduction and the first chapter part of my resume as this will establish a few points: one being that I speak from experience, the other point being that I therefore have some knowledge based on being on the inside of many a thing here. I am in fact a whistle-blower for all intents and purposes. I don't identify with this but this is a fair assessment- I am on the inside of things which many people do not even know about.

As a result I see the world around me very differently these days, and I understand the people who run our countries and world far better than I used to. This all being the result of corrupt and illegal government programs, one of which I am in, and this being the result of very corrupt and dangerous agents in my life. I have been forced into understanding the viewpoint of very corrupt and dangerous people with government job-titles, and I have witnessed for years the tactics and techniques they get away with for manipulating people and the public. I am in fact currently dealing with a psychopath with a government badge, the amount of sadistic behavior made against my family more than spells this out.

I have seen first hand how they are allowed to get away with things, how they are blindly trusted, because of a job title, a cheap stereotype that tells you nothing about what kind of people they are. I have had no choice but to learn how these type of people think, and it is uncomfortable to put one's mind into their "sewer mentality"- it is no wonder that so few people in this world understand such corrupt people. Most people are not this way, and so the average person can not relate to the mentality of corrupt and sick minded people like those within governments. The majority of people do not begin to be this way, for most this viewpoint is foreign and alien.

Again I personally have had no choice but to understand this type of person and so I hope to explain to you my reader how it is this type of person thinks and acts, their mentality and psychology, and I hope to point this out to you through observation and logic of the world around us today. I hope to show you that these people exist within our government, and to point out by example just how corrupt they are, and what they are up to. If I had not had to deal with such corrupt people, I do not think I ever would have gotten this viewpoint to the extent which I do. It took me many years and so I hope that others can therefore learn from, and benefit from my life experience. In one sense I am a whistle blower in regards to the mentality of corrupt people, and I simply step in their shoes and look at the world around me. Hopefully this book will make seeing these people, and their plans for the near future easier to identify, see, and understand. Corruption is the root of all evil, and it is what is destroying the world. Now to the adventure of my life here and my family's...

CHAPTER 1
BACK GROUND INFORMATION AND MY "CREDENTIALS"
WHAT IS CURRENTLY GOING ON IN MY LIFE: CRIMINAL
AGENTS, AND A COVER-UP : HOW DO YOU DISCREDIT THE
WITNESS SO THAT AGENCIES DO NOT INVESTIGATE ATTEMPTED
MURDER AND MURDER? YOU COMMIT ANOTHER MURDER.

For nearly twenty years now I have been dealing with a corrupt illegal government program commonly known as Mobbing and Stalking on the Internet. This all started because of two cover-ups which I knew about, one involving a pedophile police officer and the other involving a racist at 911 who deliberately delayed an ambulance because the victim was black. I was framed and put into this Mobbing.

In this Mobbing the citizens and public are misused by government agents for singling out and attacking a particular person known as the Target. It is ugly as the citizens are actually asked to do very heavy, extreme, and rude things to the Target. They are in fact by definition committing torture in an invisible form which they do not recognize, traumas, and this goes on daily for the target. They are manipulated into a "Wave" with a single mind which is controlled by the people who manipulated this Wave into being in the first place. We are talking about government agents manipulating the public into attacking an individual just like any cult or fascist movement. They are tricked into what to think, and then from there told what to do. It is sick and stupid, the citizens lose their minds. It exactly resembles how German citizens were with the Jews during the rise of Hitler, it is surreal and weird to experience. We are talking about fascism being practiced by government on a small local level, on an individual basis in regards to a particular Target. I in fact call this small portable localized movement, Localized Fascism, as that is what it is.

This government program attracts very sick agents in the first place, as you have to be to do the things that are done to people within this Stalking. It takes criminals to commit heavy crimes. This Stalking has followed me across three continents and countries, and has easily cost millions upon millions of dollars. Based on the number of agents which I have made a low guess about, the eighteen years this has gone on, and a very low estimate of 50,000 dollars a year for each agent, I estimate that more than twenty million dollars has easily been spent on me. My real guess is that it is closer to forty million. More time and man power spent on me than many a terrorist or terrorist organization. And for what and for why?

It has never made any sense to me either. I might point out here that this is one of the many reasons as to why I am writing about this, the public needs to know about this corrupt nonsense. This is your tax dollars at work, twenty to forty million of them, for and because of a pedophile and racist killer.

First the situation with the pedophile police officer happened, then a year or two later the murder. I was framed once because of the pedophile police officer, and behind my back at that for character assassination, which I remained unaware of until years later when it was brought up by these corrupt agents- who framed me in the first place. They framed me with rape (yes I assure you this is possible as I have been living the dream for twenty years), dragged my name through the dirt, and I did not even know it. This was their idea of "neutralizing" what I knew about this cover-up and pedophile police officer and later they used this behind my back for manipulating people in Stalking to attack my mental health heavily. Then later when this murder happened and I spoke out about this as well, about the man at 9/11 delaying the ambulance because the victim was black, I was framed all over again and was in fact told by one under -cover police officer directly (and emphatically), "Mind your own damn business!"- this is a direct quote. I was framed for speaking out about this and because I knew the police were doing a cover-up.

In fact this time I was framed into Stalking/Mobbing and their excuse was that I had interfered with a federal investigation which is an outright lie. It was a federal framing, I had done no such thing and they knew this as I had spoken out to many people to the contrary of what they were selling people involved in this Stalking at my job. They simply lied and took things out of context to do so, they did this with two other people I knew as well. The agents involved simply hid everything from everyone to avoid being exposed, especially from me, so they could continue to manipulate the public. If I had known then they would have been caught by me at that time. It was not until here in Europe, many years later, that I put this all together like a detective, right down to details. But back then they had everyone convinced of very many lies.

This is called programming by the way, it is an illegal misuse of psychology and a modern day form of brainwashing, and is what cults use and apparently fascist movements as well. You will note that it involves taking things out of context to trick and manipulate people into a false viewpoint and that it involves getting them to act and do things from this false viewpoint. People are given "programming sunglasses" to wear and see everything from this viewpoint, I have had everyone from close friends to parents stab me in the back because of it. Taking secret recordings out of context is standard for this, as tapes sound "real and immediate" and make taking things out of context easy- this is also the standard tool of COINTELPRO and Stalking/Mobbing. It is all in fact illegal psychology and is what cults use and is why it is illegal- it is dangerous for anyone to be doing. You will also note it involves taking things out of context which would not happen in a court room as both sides are looked at and examined; which is rather the point of court, so that this very type of thing does not happen in the first place- so that people are not falsely accused. In fact in Mobbing this is all kept away from a court room for this very reason, so that they can continue to get away with it. COINTELPRO occurs behind your back for character assassination and manipulation, Mobbing/Stalking is where it is all put out in the open and rubbed in your face. Everything about this Mobbing is highly illegal, and it is conspiracy among other things. What you have is government committing conspiracy against the people.

In order to get citizens to go along with these agents they have to be convinced that there is a legitimate cause and this is the same psychology used in creating fascist movements. People in fascist movements need a cause to solidify the movement, to create a "single mind", and so agents turn you into a "cause" for unsuspecting citizens and dupes. You are lied about and your name dragged through the dirt. People get tricked into seeing you in a way that has nothing to do with you and then once this "cements" in their mind it stays this way. Then this Fake Profile which has been sold about you, is all they see: their minds get "programmed" like a computer program, like a virus, into seeing things incorrectly. YOU become the cause and you become attacked as a result. And because of blind respect and trust for authority, this is the Trojan Horse for getting into people's minds. This is how it starts and from here they make inroads until your mind is on a string for them to pull.

Since it is as easy as lying and having a government badge I can safely say it does not take much for people to be convinced that there is a legitimate cause. The cause being a matter of character assassination. This most certainly is how it has been in my life and this is why these agents have kept things out of court. Everything they have lied about and taken out of context would be exposed and put back into it's proper place and perspective-which is something that corrupt agents do not want. It looks bad for their business if the public finds out that it is being lied to and misused for attacking an innocent person. That said these citizens have no business doing what they are doing in the first place, and I am no more "their Jew", than Jews were during the time of Hitler, if you get my point. If you can not then maybe that is part of the problem.

The reality is that these citizens would not be taking part in any of this if they knew what this is really all about, a pedophile police officer and a racist killer at 911. How many would? Again the truth has to be hidden from the public.

Many people I have dealt with in my life simply assumed that I must have done something horrible for all of this time, money, and manpower to be wasted on me. Their "logic" to the insanity of this is, "Well why else would they be doing it?", like this explains something. And of course the real answer is "If there is a reason, then why have they not pressed charges?", and "Why do I continue to be followed around and harassed?", and "They need to conduct a twenty year investigation across three countries and continents?", those are the real answers. We can also toss in at this point, "Why are they attacking my family then?" which again points to the Truth. Another good one is "Why have they killed two of our pets then?" as this says something as well, doesn't it? I have deliberately never been charged so they can continue to get away doing what they are doing. In court it all falls down. Thus it has all remained out of court, it is simple. They have had to lie and manipulate, they have had to take things out of context to even have a pretense and excuse for citizens in the first place. What citizens do not know is what they get away with. As long as no one listens, asks questions, digs deep enough to find out the truth, then no one will know. And they are told to not ask questions and told lies about why you say things- it is all about appearances.

These agents do not want your name cleared, and they do not want to be seen for what they are: they are criminal and involved in an illegal government program in the first place.

CURRENT CIRCUMSTANCES HERE IN EUROPE
CORRUPT PROGRAMS, CORRUPT AGENTS, CORRUPT MESSES

Now to the present time then a look at the bigger picture in regards to this Stalking. This book is about many different pieces of which this Stalking is one piece, and this book is about what these pieces make as a bigger picture. This book is about the people behind the scenes who are hiding this bigger picture as well. It is all about corruption, corrupt people, and their plans for America, their countries, and the world. That which ties and connects these pieces is corruption and corrupt minds. This chapter is to give background information, history, and to establish that which makes me qualified on a few points here. It is also for the protection of my family as you will see.

In regards to me I have never been in a position to take these people to court because of finances, but I am now starting to look for lawyers. I am in fact being forced into this because the agents involved are extremely corrupt and dangerous and have gotten away with a cover-up by being so convincing that agencies of this land felt "no need" to investigate. And this is after I had contacted them about attempted murder. Because these agents are dangerous and because agencies are doing nothing I am forced into this, and as a result of agencies not performing their jobs responsibly and competently. They have been tricked with simple misdirection from the beginning into believing in a profile I do not have and into believing that this so called "profile" is a result of Mobbing, which it is not. It is a result of manipulation, technology, and part of a strategy for a cover-up, and if agencies had contacted witnesses they would have found this out. Who fakes or pretends to have witnesses? No one does as most agencies have the brains to contact witnesses in the first place, therefore lying about such is stupid.

Agencies have been tricked into looking at Mobbing instead of looking at agents doing a cover-up. Last time I checked this is called misdirection. Pretty simple, it has tricked multiple agencies around here. I and my family thank you for your support, and it is not my fault that my girlfriend is too afraid to speak out, it is no wonder. She sees that I am speaking out, and sees the reward of no one believing, never mind all of the deliberate attacks made against her for the last two years to condition her hard core into keeping her mouth shut- talk about surreal. In the meantime let me point out that if this Stalking were not going on, and if technology were not being misused heavily, agencies would already have investigated and caught these people.

These corrupt agents I deal with most certainly are not about agencies, not even their own, and they most certainly are not about this Mobbing. They act independently of both. If their agency and agencies of this land knew the truth, they would be going after these agents (minus "politics" of the Clown's agency and the problems created here- like it is my fault) as they are a threat to anyone, that is rather the point. These agents are no more loyal to their agency than they are to any other, they are corrupt and self-serving. These agents in particular are every bad cliché of their agency and they would stab anyone in the back for their own butts, they already have. They are a gang of cheap killers and cowards that is exactly what they are and in many ways they are a smaller version of this Elite.

They get that this program is corrupt and they are making the most of it and their job titles for themselves, they are like many a corrupt politician. They get to live like gods with no accountability and do whatever they want. During my first book "Don't Tread On Me" and while they did everything they could to interfere with it and stop it, they attempted murder of a citizen after communicating as much to me first, then it happened- all as a way of trying to scare me into stopping my book. Since they did not stop me, they began attacking it in other ways, this involving exotic government technology, and quite frankly it is a non-sellable mess. In the meantime another murder was committed this year in March 2012 three days before I was going to send cassettes to agencies which would have opened an investigation, and this one was to discredit me, go figure. I live in the only land in the world where agencies do not investigate, do not contact or interview witnesses, and where the killers are given the benefit of the doubt while they commit another murder as a way of doing a cover-up. Somehow I expected agencies to do better than this.

In the meantime I have multiple witnesses to the fact that they stopped my book for two years, which they used for coming up with a strategy and cover-up, and they sold my witnesses various lies and stories for about one and a half years, which were all DIFFERENT from the lie they are now selling. In other words these agents realized they needed a different lie and story in place for their cover-up, and so later when they realized this, they changed their story and are now selling something totally different. This is one thing of very many things that agencies remain unaware of.

Thus for the sake of my own protection and my family's I will have to get loud before I can even take agencies to court- and if they can not do their jobs responsibly. Last time I checked I and my family are witnesses which can have these people put in prison which means I have no choice, I have safety and survival issues here for me and my family, never mind torture issues. I and my family each know enough to get these people investigated. I quite literally have to get a lawyer to get these people to do their jobs, and at some point will have to hire someone to interview witnesses and to present agencies with the truth of everything here since they could not "waste their time" finding out. Generally speaking interviewing witnesses is a good place to start and this Mobbing is the only situation in which normal protocols are not followed. Coincidence? This Mobbing is in fact being used as a cover story for performing a cover-up without looking suspicious. It really makes you wonder how good agencies are at their own business.

It has taken a long time to reach this point of getting a lawyer, and the agent in charge, Horbat (fictional name) a.k.a. the Clown, has been hiding her corruption for many years. Quite obviously agencies have never caught on, yet are inches from catching these people while they continue to remain clueless. Again more corrupt agents in my life, and these are just as dirty as the ones who framed me into this Mobbing back in America. We are talking about a cold blooded psychopath doing things in terms of strategy to avoid being caught for corruption and murder yet no one from agencies has even caught on. No one has even looked. And these people are supposed to be protecting the public and people, well take a good look.

This should give you an idea of the intelligence of agencies, government, and illegal government programs.

And these are the things which are supposed to be protecting you. It is ALL about corruption. Corrupt programs attract corrupt agents and this mess, my life and my family's, is a result of corruption. This is how, where, and why I have the credentials that I do. I have been forced into understanding the mentality and viewpoint of the people I am dealing with, and specifically the Clown who is a psychopath. And it is very uncomfortable to do but since I am dealing with killers and since I have family, I am forced into doing this. I have had no choice.

To add to all of this crazy mess, these corrupt agents have been discrediting me with a type of classified technology in regards to agencies (think of this in terms of fake tapes) so that the Clown remains uncaught. This Clown literally revealed this classified information and technology to me and my family and parents, and it is so heavily misused, there is no denying it's existence. So while I am discredited heavily these agents go free. It is almost as if they would do anything with their technology, like say discredit the witness and sell an artificial profile to avoid being caught.... And ironically enough the obvious signs of a cover-up are all around, along with the obvious signs of this woman's profile which is that she is a psychopath. Currently everything resembles an episode of "Hogan's Heros".

I am extremely concerned by what is being done and agencies remain clueless, thus this particular chapter with the story of what is going on as well. It is all connected and inter-related, it is all about corruption and the misuse of power.

Take a look at the following chapters within, like a detective anyone can look at these pieces and see how they all fit together, anyone can see that the motives of these Elite are not for good and not for security, it is in fact not difficult to see this nor is it difficult to get the mentality of these corrupt Elite. I feel I do a fairly good job in getting this viewpoint across to people through a variety of chapters, I certainly hope so at any rate.

Corruption is the root of all evil in our times and it is about time that something was done about it. It is about time for the people to wake-up and recognize what is the real threat to our country and world. It is about time that people focused on the real issue destroying countries from within, it is about time that the real criminals were held responsible and caught, it is about time that people realize what they have in common, and it is about time that the people declared A War Against Corruption instead of being divided amongst themselves. People should be going after those making misery in their lives and this world, not after each other. People need to change their consciousness on an individual level, and once this has happened a New Revolution will begin, a Path of Consciousness.

CHAPTER 2
LOBBYING IN AMERICA

Lobbying is INSTITUTIONALIZED-BRIBERY, institutionalized corruption. The American people have an issue with this, as well they should, yet never seem to speak of this problem for what it is. Lobbying is a deliberate mislabeling, a tactic, to conceal the truth- lobbying is institutionalized bribery, corruption. Put it clearly and it should not even be an issue- bribery is bribery. Once people start dealing with this issue more accurately, start speaking of it for what it is, the problem itself will not be as hidden, and can be dealt with in a more truthful manner. It will be seen for the deceit and lie it is. Who came up with the term lobbying? Obviously politicians and companies, the people engaging in this who wanted the name changed to something less obvious. The people need to start labeling this problem for what it is and confronting the politicians with this fact: bribery is bribery and corruption is corruption. Which politician is going to claim that lobbying is a good thing, or a necessary thing, or a part of the process, once it is identified for what it is? No politician is going to claim that bribery is a good thing or a necessary thing, or a part of the process once it has been identified for what it is. If the American people really want to fix this problem then they need to address it for what it is...Plain and simple, see how quickly the reading goes with me?

CHAPTER 3
GUANTANAMO BAY

An experiment, public profiling, a test case and field-testing, to check public apathy in regards to concentration camps and torture. If your government can get away with torturing "others" they can get away with torturing YOU. Their rights are your rights. In a democracy we should hold our standards higher, and if not, are we really acting as a democracy?...

CHAPTER 4
WATER-BOARDING– IS IT TORTURE?

This next piece which I wrote several years ago came about as a result of being sick of hearing such an obviously ridiculous question being paraded by various media outlets as a subject of serious philosophical debate. If you know anyone that is thickheaded on this subject maybe this will help wake them up. I consider this piece a good example of how the public is manipulated, and quite obviously is not directed at my readers.

Is water boarding torture?

This question is sheer nonsense, junk-for-the-mind, a total distraction from the truth of the matter. An insult to the intelligence of the masses and sold to us by corrupt people trying to make torture more acceptable. If this subject is questionable for you, then I hope I clear things up for you.

It's torture when you EXPERIENCE it. Do you think it is an issue for the people who experience it? If it remains a question in your mind then you are trying to look intelligent because that's the question you've heard over and over in the media, and because it is acceptable to question such an obvious thing. In fact it "looks" intelligent to do so. Having said that, if that is the case for you, for actual intelligent people you do not look very bright here. If you are going to be intelligent, you need to think intelligently, as opposed to looking it. Water boarding has only become an issue of torture because of the media, until that time no one would even think to consider it anything but torture. In fact until that time, before that time, if you had brought this up as an issue of debate and consideration people would have thought you were nuts for doing so. People are allowing themselves to be manipulated by the media on this point. It ought to be clear. Water boarding is literally the act of being drowned, how pleasant do you think it is? How normal do you think it is that this is being brought up as a subject of debate by the media? What are the motives here?

This is fake-objectivity, this is media-objectivity, this is fake media objectivity. It is trying to find truth inside of a false and incorrect answer- it is philosophizing for the sake of philosophizing. It is an insult to intelligent conscious people and a joke perpetrated on the masses. You can forget it as even being an issue if you can think for yourself. People who see the truth of this issue practice independent-thinking, people who see such an issue as a matter of consideration and debate think what they are told to think, which is what television is all about.

How hard is it to imagine on your end?

The only part of you questioning water-boarding is your ego and how society might react, what society might think if you do not contemplate the issue. Because society has also had the same mantra repeated down it's throat. You are worried about what other like-minded people might think. You're worried about what others think, not what the truth is. The TRUTH is what ought to be your focus and concern here. Your worries are externalized, not internalized. Externalized is what others think, internalized is, "What if it was me?". This last question IS the answer. Water boarding feels like drowning because you are drowning when it is being done to you; how hard is this to see as the torture it is? Fake-objectivity comes from the outside-in, and is a matter of considering a false viewpoint because it has been crammed down your throat so many times. It is in fact programming which is a subtle form of brainwashing. Any viewpoint of common sense gets thrown out the window and substituted for a different one that someone else wants you to wear: because it is beneficial to them. One clear indicator of programming is that many times when you look you see that common sense has been thrown out the window. Like say how hard is it to see that water boarding is torture?..

This is divide and conquer with the masses, plus an insult to the intelligence of all.

To quote something I heard on the B.B.C. from someone in a foreign land who used to torture people: "Torture is the art of killing a man without him dying.", and that is what water boarding is. And it is what I have been experiencing for eighteen years now, and my family for ten years.

CHAPTER 5
ARE YOU DIVIDED BY POLITICAL PARTIES? PEOPLE NEED TO FOCUS ON THE ROOT PROBLEM OF AMERICA WHICH IS CORRUPTION IN GOVERNMENT AND THE APATHY OF THE MASSES: HOW ABOUT A WAR AGAINST CORRUPTION?

Folks if we are going to live in a democracy then we are going to have to take responsibility for it. This means making sure that our representatives are doing their job as they are meant to. This means making sure our representatives are actually servants of the people. Turning a blind-eye, being apathetic, accepting what is wrong with our land and with our people, accepting what is wrong with our government and representatives, will not work. Acceptance is a great thing when it is genuine and appropriate, but when it is used to hide laziness of the mind, and apathy, it is not.

If we are going to live in a democracy then we must be vigilant, fight for it, and protect it. Corruption is a sign of decay, of a downward spiral for any country or empire, history speaks of this. Corruption is a sign of any countries downfall. When we have representatives that actually do their job properly, who actually represent the people and America, and not themselves (corruption), then we will have a country that functions properly and more smoothly. Is there any doubt to this statement?

Politicians are the one group of people where the letters of the law, justice, ought to be served, yet strangely enough these people are held the least accountable within our land. Think this is a coincidence? You have to be blind to think that it is. And these people are responsible for writing laws and representing our people. How intelligent are we as a people for allowing this to happen? How intelligent do we look to the rest of the world? Until people get over political boundaries, and start focusing on the real issue, corruption, things will never change. People need to start working together, need to unite, and start dealing with this problem, taking our country back from the corrupt politicians. Corrupt politicians being a party unto themselves who represent themselves, and who have hijacked America for their own personal gain. As long as we remain divided on this issue, blaming it on political parties, not on corrupt-individuals, they will continue to get away and misuse our country. The ROOT PROBLEM needs to be focused on and addressed here. If you cut off the head the body will die. Corruption, A War Against Corruption, needs to be the issue for the people. Corruption exists on both sides of the fence. Political parties and their ideals are not the issue, weak-minded greedy-people are. When you focus on the real-issue, there is no divided people. How can there be, who wants corruption and corrupt politicians?

I recommend A War Against Corruption, within America which will clean our country up. As opposed to a war on drugs which will further divide the American people and allow the real criminals to get away. Generally speaking corrupt people are involved in the dealing of large amounts of drugs and transporting them, for money and power as an example. You can not clean up drug problems or anything else until you clean up corruption within government. How about A War Against Corruption? This will unify the people around what is really destroying America, and clean America up making her a respected nation again. This applies to all other countries as well.

CHAPTER 6
DEMOCRACY AND PSEUDO-DEMOCRACY

Democracy is when power and the sharing and entitlement of power is spread out amongst the individuals, the masses. Not when it is hoarded at the top of the societal food chain: the rich, the corporations, the corrupt, the Elite. And not when its an exclusive club whose main requirement is being corrupt. This is why more and more government is being centralized, it's to put the power in the hands of the few and to take away what little is left for the masses, from the masses. Last time I checked police-states had this kind of power structure for this very reason. Funny how people remain blind though, huh? The power structure within American government is changing. The Constitution, the people's protection, is being over run by corrupt people who want more power by consolidating power, yet since the country still wears the label of democracy, well then it must be so. Is everyone blind? The label of democracy for America is inaccurate these days, false, as in a lie. Until the people actually retake an interest in the quality of their representatives, and the quality of their country, reclaiming their responsibility for democracy, it will remain so. The inside is being eaten away by corruption, while the surface remains the same: like a tree being eaten away by termites. Until American's do so, reclaim their responsibility for democracy, it is just the shell of democracy that is left- appearances and looks until the tree finally breaks.

CHAPTER 7
THE AMERICAN GOVERNMENT AND THE AMERICAN CONSTITUTION

The difference between the American government and the American Constitution is that government servants, government is replaceable, THE CONSTITUTION IS NOT. There is something wrong with the politicians, not the constitution. When the system fails in America, and it will by design (Folks we are reaching a point where we can not pay the interest on the national debt), there should not be an emotional reaction from the public as this will justify martial law, but there should be a call for the entire replacement of government employees, ie. politicians. When the entire system in America crashes, this will be a result of corrupt politicians, not a result of the Constitution. Amongst all of them only a few are honest, and/or, not looking the other way due to fear of the corrupt and powerful amongst them. How about more honest politicians with more back bone? How's that for a solution? In the end it is the only thing that will restore faith in the American system and America itself world wide. Again, any failings in America have to do with the quality of the politicians, not the Constitution. Any failings of America have to do with the people being apathetic, not taking action, in regards to the up-keep of their country.

CHAPTER 8
THE DIFFERENCE BETWEEN A PATRIOT AND NATIONALIST:
"WE THE PEOPLE" VS. "WE THE GOVERNMENT"

Being a patriot means putting the Constitution first, being a nationalist means putting government first. The Constitution, people, and country, should always come first. Without these basics the whole thing can fall apart due to corruption... Being a patriot means believing in ideals which are infallible (like freedom), being a nationalist means believing in people, politicians, who are quite fallible. Imagine that... To a very large extent, it is a fair case to say that it is a matter of those who are self-empowered vs those who are not self-empowered. The difference between those who think on their own, vs. those who want to be told what to think, and what to do. Keep this statement in mind, I will get to it later. But as a hint and point, the Terrorism Scare is the Red Scare all over again, and because people are being non-thinking, simply reacting out of fear and doing what they are told.

CHAPTER 9
CORRUPTION: A NEW DEFINITION TO BE CONSIDERED, A MENTAL DISEASE, A MENTAL-DISORDER

Corruption: a mental disease that eats individuals, cultures, societies, and countries from within. Do I mean literally a mental disease like schizophrenia? Yes as a matter of fact I do, and it's about time that this was, and is considered. However like the common cold or influenz it can spread from person-to-person, whichever person that it makes contact with. How strong is your own immune system? The final stage of any society, culture, and country is corruption. Corruption always eats away at the very system, culture, society, and country it exists within until it implodes. Like a tree being eaten from within by insects, it looks fine until everything breaks and implodes at once due to the decay, corruption within. Take a good look at America and the world, ask yourself how much time is left.

CHAPTER 10
GUANTANAMO BAY PART 2: A TEST-CASE AND PUBLIC-PROFILING TO CHECK PUBLIC APATHY IN REGARDS TO TORTURE AND CONCENTRATION CAMPS

Guantanamo Bay is a test case, a profiling of the American peoples psyche, in regards to torture and prison-camps. It's that plain and simple. It's also to acclimate and desensitize the American people to the idea of torture camps because that is what it is. No doubt there are more in store for America, and these are called Custodial Facilities by the American government.

How many people in Guantanamo Bay are actually guilty? I doubt very many. Financial incentives were and are offered as an incentive for turning people in. This creates a greed witch hunt atmosphere. Under such circumstances people will turn in people they don't like, even their neighbors or total strangers for a change in life style and a few perks along the way, it's called GREED. The people initiating this witch hunt know this, they have their own goals and objectives which are also greedy. Thus they spread the wealth based on human weakness, based on greed, which is a weakness of the mind. It is a corruption of the mind and in this case they are using it to get results which benefit them.

It's a dumb way to go about catching bad guys, especially when in this case no real proof was needed. It's not like these people were going to court. But it is a good way of obtaining a lot of people whether they are guilty or not. It is a good way of obtaining instant results, a good way of obtaining a lot of people whether they are guilty or not, a good way of obtaining numbers, which looks good to the American public eye. This is about appearances. Never letting these people go to court maintains the lie. None of this is coincidence.

It is in fact a farce and a lie, never mind the injustice.

This is why a lot of terrorist cases keep popping up in the public eye in America: to maintain a farce. Greedy informants and morally misaligned federal agents, corrupt agents (obviously not all- but applicable to these particular circumstances), are acting out of greed and ego, targeting a certain group of people, or individuals, and encouraging them with ideas and statements to break the law. Time and again it is the informants leading the charge with these individuals. Never mind outright lying by these informants. These informants get thousands of dollars as a result. Are we talking about "ideals" here, or greed and the type of dishonest person that comes with it? Many of these informants are filthy.

These informants are actually encouraging and promoting terrorism for their bank account, because of greed. The Feds, morally misaligned, in turn get to look good. This is how Ruby Ridge happened as an example. This is why a lot of these cases make a media sensation but then later fall flat on their face in court. But you don't hear the media sensation on those cases when they fall flat on their face, do you? When the Truth of the matter comes out, you do not hear about that. Take a look, it's the initial farce that receives the attention not the revelation of Truth later, of what it is, that gets the attention. Again it is about what is on the surface- what looks good and what sounds good in the moment. This is a matter of programming the masses. Reality and the truth get ignored when it does not fit this government and media agenda. When you see the mainstream-media practicing such a lack of objectivity we have to begin to question the media, never mind the issues of water boarding. Clearly the mainstream media is being used and misused to affect and steer the thinking and thoughts of the masses. The media is being used to affect the perceptions of the masses, this is called programming and programming is a form of modern day brainwashing, a very insidious and subtle form. This is what propaganda is on many a fine point.

The mistakes made and the incorrectness of parading around people who are "guilty" when we later find out they are NOT, is never as popular with the media. The mistake of it all never receives as much attention. Quite obviously the mainstream media is corrupt and controlled and incapable of practicing objectivity with others, with non-guilty people and with itself. When they do acknowledge that terrorist suspects were not actually guilty, it is brief and fleeting to protect the system. It is mentioned a few moments no doubt so they can claim objectivity without actually practicing it. And afterwards you do not see the media going after the system, people, and processes which happened and which led to innocent people being charged. They make a big sensation when everything looks good without having all of the facts, but when the Truth comes out and we find out it was all a farce then they barely mention it. The whole thing is a scam, farce, and lie. Both government and the media are guilty here, and the masses are misled. A lot of what is going on resembles the Red Scare and it is no coincidence. This is all being done deliberately to generate hype for a perpetual sales pitch to the public: to maintain fear for obtaining compliance of the public.

I know what a farce this is from my own life and the government agents in it. These government agents have three basic rules as they have communicated to me. Rule one: first us then the target. This means how they look in any situation comes first regardless of truth. Rule two: how do we make it (any given situation) work for us? Rule three: if it works it is good. It's pretty cut and dry isn't it ? No morals or ethics there but it does give you a very good basic idea of these people and their rules of thumb. Being good and doing the right thing doesn't even begin to enter the picture with these people. These people lack morals and ethics and everyone else is an inanimate object to them. Of course I speak of corrupt agents here, I have met more than a few during nearly two decades of my Mobbing who were good and about doing the right thing.

As I was saying I know what a sick joke it is from my own life. As usual the agents get to look good and the public is deceived. This has been used repeatedly in my life.

CHAPTER 11
COINTELPRO- COUNTER INTELLIGENCE PROGRAM: DECLARED ILLEGAL YET IT LIVES ON TO THIS DAY: MOBBING, STALKING, STREET THEATER- THE NEXT LEVEL OF COINTELPRO, ANOTHER ILLEGAL GOVERNMENT PROGRAM FOR GREATER CONTROL OF THE CITIZENS:
PROGRAMMIMG, THE ILLEGAL PSYCHOLOGY MISUSED IN THESE PROGRAMS FOR GREATER CONTROL:
HOW THESE PROGRAMS ALL FIT A BIGGER PICTURE

"Fascism is when government becomes cult"- Mr. Lee

COINTELPRO, standing for Counter Intelligence Program, was exposed in 1971 by activists who raided a FBI office and stole many of their files. Eventually there was an investigation into this information and program- COINTELPRO was officially exposed. This turned out to be a very good thing as COINTELPRO was exposed for the corrupt and dirty program it was and is, and supposedly it was ended. It however was not, it obviously was renamed and hidden all over again, a common government tactic.

Obviously those within government responsible for this program wanted and want the power and control which comes from it, as it is criminal and corrupt and as it continues on. From personal experience I can tell you that it was not ended and I can tell you that it also happens to be one of the biggest waste of tax dollars on the planet. It is a huge waste of money, corrupt, and is illegal for very good reason.

Now this program COINTELPRO was all about targeting individuals and destroying them. It was and is the misuse of the legal system for destroying a chosen target. Currently this is what is being done to Julian Assange of WikiLeaks, he is in fact dealing with COINTELPRO. I would know as I too experienced COINTELPRO beginning in the early 1990s, and as I continue to experience the tactics of it to this day. In fact COINTELPRO is about the creation of government gangs who acted and act just as hard core criminal gangs would and do, but even worse as in this case they are given the power of government. It takes hard core criminals to commit hard core crimes and this is what COINTELPRO does. We are talking about the government hiring hard-core criminals to attack citizens here,

We are talking about the creation of government gangs who target those who are out spoken and therefore a threat to the system. ALL high profile cases become targets of COINTELPRO. COINTELPRO is the defensive and offensive weapon for a corrupt system created by corrupt politicians. This was allowed and instituted by corrupt politicians who want to protect their base of power. The system is in effect targeting individuals early on before they become a big problem, and neutralizing them before they acquire power and become a threat to corrupt politicians, which IS the system. It is about making sure that there are no more Martin Luther Kings, no more Gandhis.

It is about making sure that their power remains centralized and unchallenged, and more importantly than that making sure that no one is able to challenge what they want. It is about making sure that no individual obtains a level of power which is a threat to them and the system they have created for their greater power and control. Thus activists and potential leaders are targeted from the beginning. These illegal programs target anyone trying to do the right thing, who go against corruption. Is this American?

We are talking about gangs who are trained in agency tactics and psychology, who have government badges and who are given permission and authority to destroy the target, and through all means: including assassination, murder. In fact COINTELPRO can be summed up in this one word alone-assassination, whether it be physical assassination or character assassination. There was and is nothing too low for COINTELPRO and the agents within it, it was all about destroying people and even framing people or killing them. In order to do this you need agents who are criminal, corrupt, dangerous, and psychotic. It goes without saying that you need murderers to do the job of murdering. You have to be sick to kill and to label someone a rapist.

How is that for a government program? I have had 18 years of Stalking as a result of this sick program.

Needless to say there was a public backlash to it's exposure, it was declared finished and over but like all government programs that give a lot of power to government and corrupt politicians within it, it was never stopped but was simply re-hidden. I say that based on my life and this Stalking as it is called on the Internet and this program is obviously a step above COINTELPRO. COINTELPRO is what I was dealing with BEFORE I ended up in this Mobbing- COINTELPRO and corrupt agents are in fact what put me in this program of Mobbing. Basically Mobbing is carried on out in the open in front of the target, whereas COINTELPRO is carried out behind the scenes for destroying the target. But the point is they are very similar and one exists in the shadows, the other out in the open, in the light of day so to speak. And based on my life I find that it is safe to say that BOTH programs are becoming more prolific and accepted by a clueless public.

Now COINTELPRO was originally created in 1956 for investigating and attacking communist parties within America during the Red Scare. Based on what I am experiencing in my life now because of this similar program, I find it interesting. As currently the Terrorism Scare of our times is the exact same thing as the Red Scare, and as the Patriot Act is simply a hidden form of COINTELPRO. It is the Red Scare all over again, it is the SAME game plan being used here- it is the same strategy.

The Patriot Act in fact brings COINTELPRO one step closer to being accepted and legal. Really the Patriot Act is COINTELPRO in disguise- it enables all of the same violations of one's rights. Corrupt politicians are moving it one step closer to being in the open and acceptable because they are trying to slowly acclimate and de-sensitize the public in regards to these dangerous and illegal programs. Look at the wording of the Patriot Act and switch the word "patriot" for "terrorist", and you begin to get an idea. In fact the Patriot Act states who it targets in the name of the Act itself, the Patriot Act targets patriots. It is about corrupt powerful people wanting to control the population through a hidden form of fascism, COINTELPRO and Mobbing, as fascism and cult go hand in hand. A people controlled in this way are non-thinking and simply doing what they are told by government agents: I would know I have experienced this for almost twenty years. People all across the world are these days, it is an international conspiracy. If it does not exist then governments should not be faking it. This COINTELPRO is being conducted all across the world, the evidence is all over the Internet.

As the governments across the world prepare for world shocks and traumas (MK Ultra on a global scale), they want a population that is indoctrinated into doing what it is told by government. They are preparing for an economic crash or some other world shock, and New World Order which no doubt will be declared the solution - one world government, and a one world economic system. And in my opinion it will most likely be an economy crash. And when that time of an economy crash comes, our politicians and media will remind us that "Obviously capitalism does not work" the same as was heard about the Soviet Union and how "Communism does not work". This will be the new mantra and sales pitch for getting what they want. The problem and lie here is that capitalism does work it is just that corrupt politicians across the world have robbed America and other lands blind. This COINTELPRO fits in with all of this as they want a population that is tightly controlled so that they do not have to worry about consequences.

I have traveled across three countries and continents, America, Europe, and Asia (India- Herakhan), and this program of Mobbing has FOLLOWED ME all of the way and for almost twenty years now. So I know first hand that this has been agreed upon by all governments. This Mobbing is simply a different form of COINTELPRO, it is all very much the same. Now look at why. It is about controlling the people tightly through blind respect for authority, fanaticism/fascism, so that when these governments become public with things like an economy crash there will already be a large part of the population that is compliant to government, it is so corrupt government has less to worry about, this is exactly what this is about. It is about tricking the public into giving up total control, it is about programming the masses.

As a point there is an old text supposedly written by the Elite more than a hundred years ago, "The Protocols of Zion", and one would normally think this is all false kooky bologne until you see that their plans and intended goals are all obviously happening during our times. The first time I discovered this I was surprised, it is too much to be coincidence. In this text they state that their goal is to have one in three serving the government as spies and informants, these programs of COINTELPRO and Stalking serve this very purpose. This is "Obama's Citizen Police Force". Coincidence?

Fascism is when government becomes cult and that is exactly how people are in this Stalking and COINTELPRO. And you will note that these programs are becoming prolific across the world because of this. Because governments have been indoctrinating their people into fascism and it is spreading like a Wave, it is corruption of the mind. If citizens are not being trained to blindly serve government then they should not be pretending to mob me because of a pedophile police officer. But what do I know, maybe they respect his badge.

THE "CITIZEN POLICE FORCE" AND FUTURE

When something happens on a world scale the people will be divided and many will be turning on others for a pat on the back from government, just like many people do to me now without even really knowing what it is all about. It will be like Hitler's time, many will lose their heads and act stupidly here on behalf of government. Based on my own experience with this government program of Mobbing I would say that many already are and have. That is the whole point, the groundwork for this army of non-thinking people is already being laid down, whistle-blowers are being targeted heavily by these programs as they are the first defense of people's rights. Corrupt people from the beginning want good people and whistle blowers out of the way, it is all about a deliberate strategy. COINTELPRO is a very large part of this, it is everything.

If you also look at the No Fly List, the planned shut down of the Internet in 2012, Custodial Facilities (aka prisons) across America, these illegal programs, then you see that this all fits together. ALL of this points to preparation by governments against their own populations in regards to an unseen event. Instead of informing the public of what will occur and happen, the governments across the world are simply planning. They are in fact preparing for the locking up and over-throw of their own people. It is all about to turn into "We the Government" instead of "We the People".

Now so far governments are not stating honestly that a world economy crash will happen (There are basic economic realities here Folks), so far they are only putting band-aides on everything, talking about spending cuts etc, without actually doing anything. They are selling people false hope until a crash happens, they have no intention of doing anything. They have put more time and energy into preparations for the over-throw of the people rather than into fixing the problems themselves which would ever lead to such an event in the first place. This has a lot to do with why the government has built Custodial Facilities all across America instead of speaking openly with the people. And no matter what you call a prison, a prison is a prison, it remains the same thing regardless of it's name.

So if you do not accept their solutions and cures but if you manage to avoid rioting- rioting is what they want so they have an excuse for martial law, and manage to avoid being put in a custodial facility, then perhaps you will be taken to one later once they have their system of a Citizen Police Force activated. What you will have is a bunch of brainless non-thinking citizens turning in people they do not like and who they suspect based on this. This

Citizen Police Force will be a nightmare. In fact Obama made references to this Citizen Police Force (2010?), and this is what he was talking about. It was a direct reference to this program of Stalking and COINTELPRO. So many people who have heard of Mobbing or who taken part in it, just do not realize that there is a much bigger picture here. The bigger plan of COINTELPRO and Mobbing, what they are pieces of, is the creation of a world police-state. It is a global agreement for laying down the groundwork of fascism. It is all about this New World Order, one centralized government, the consolidation of power at the top of the food chain.

This Elite have drained all of many countries resources quite deliberately and now they plan on taking more power and control rather than be caught. They are taking a negative situation that they have created and are now making it work for themselves all over again.

GANG STALKING, MOBBING, PROGRAMMING THE PUBLIC-ILLEGAL PSYCHOLOGY

What I go through, Stalking/ Mobbing, is a government program and one which is about creating compliance to government authority. Both in regards to citizens and the target, and for each group a different psychology is used. One involves torture and traumas to get compliance from the target and the other involves the psychology involved in creating fascist movements to get compliance from the citizens. The tactics of MK-Ultra (another illegal program that was exposed) is misused against the target to traumatize and harass the target into compliance, and the public is misused to do this through "programming". Programming is in fact modern day brain washing, it is in fact more subtle and insidious: it is also what cults use, and the psychology is ILLEGAL: except apparently if you are a government agent trained in it and misusing it on the public.

Below is a piece of writing on programming the public from my book "Don't Tread On Me" which was put out in a hurry because of corrupt government agents threatening to kill me and because they killed a second one of our pets. This first book needs major editing work and it was spiked heavily by agents and technology, but the knowledge within it is good, especially if you are in this Mobbing. Again I was in a hurry at the time never mind other issues such as technology being misused to create problems with my writing (and this is still a problem) This book you read now is in fact mostly from "Don't Tread On Me", except for this chapter which is added, some well needed editing (it still needs more), and with the tin foil hat chapters removed.

Now before I move on here I would like to say that if you think I am making this all up about Stalking what am I supposed to say? I and my family are insiders in regards to this government program, and I experience all of this regardless of what you believe. That is rather the point, it is up to people like me to inform the public which needs to know about these programs and needs to be aware of them so that it can all be exposed and stopped. Otherwise from my perspective the entire scenario is a waste of an experience never mind tax dollars. I try to make good of it all by exposing it and making the public conscious about it. Again I am an insider and no one is in denial about other things which are exposed by whistle blowers, so why should that be the case here?

As more people speak out the more positive action and energy that is put into going against it, the greater the chance of this being exposed and stopped. It is about physics, the law of cause and effect, a balancing of energy, what I call Human Physics. This is what motivates me, now look at the motivations and methods used here by the people who thought these laws and programs up. These things are most certainly not about freedom or democracy, they are about power and control, fascism, illegal laws, and ultimately about creating a police state. The energy is negative, it is plain to see. The entire focus of these programs is about more power, while democracy is the sharing of power, which these illegal programs are the opposite of. These programs are in fact attacking democracy, and if you live in America, attacking the Constitution. No democracy can borrow measures from a police state and then claim to be about democracy, this much should be clear. It ought to be equally clear that I am writing from experience here and that I have no rights at all along with my family. And what is done to us can be done to you, our rights are your rights.

I feel it is important that the public becomes aware of how government does these things and "programming" is a major part of this- without programming these illegal programs can not function. This programming is heavily and constantly used in Stalking and COINTELPRO every single day and you can even see this being done in the media. Again programming is modern day brainwashing- but much more subtle, it is what cults use and it is dangerous for a reason. We are talking about government misusing this sick psychology for manipulating a Wave of people into attacking a fellow citizen in very nasty ways that none of these people would want done to themselves. For a current example of Gang Stalking see Randy Quaid and what has been happening in his life, and for a really good example of how COINTELPRO works see the current life of Julian Assange from WikiLeaks, it does not take much to be labeled a rapist. These are two good current examples.

Now to programming the public, and as you will note this piece also gives a very good idea of what Stalking is all about- how nasty and illegal it all is. This is in fact a snapshot from my life and my family's. I hope that by exposing this that I am able to neutralize it to some extent.

Keep in mind that the target can be chosen from a variety of reasons: in my case I was framed because of a pedophile police officer and murdering racist, it does not take much to get in this Mobbing. If you are not alarmed by my circumstances you should be. And it is safe to say based on a very low estimate of the amount of agents and their pay checks, and almost twenty years of this, that more than 20 million dollars has been spent on all of this so far. And I am only one person. Your tax dollars at work, take a good look at what your dollars are being spent on...Talk about surreal.

AN EXAMPLE OF PROGRAMMING THE PUBLIC AND INDIVIDUALS: HOW PROGRAMMED PEOPLE AND "WHAT THEY EXPERIENCE" IS NOT REALITY, AND IS NOT CORRECT: HOW AGENTS CREATE FAKE WITNESSES FROM PROGRAMMED PEOPLE

The public began targeting my kid at the age of two. These Spooks sold this as helping me out with my "sensitivity" in regards to my kid, life, and people, which was a lie and farce. This was a lie and cover story.

The first time this happened was at the playground, I was with my kid, the two of us alone except for a woman walking by which I did not see at the time. My kid was looking in her direction and began crying for no reason. I turned quickly and saw this woman stop what she was doing but not before I saw what was happening- she was pointing a finger accusingly at my kid and making all of these facial gestures like she was extremely angry at my kid. Of course my kid was scared and I was shocked- this woman quickly walked away while I was still in shock. Who does this, what type of person does this to a two year old? Well let's look at some points here.

In real life and context, a disturbed person does this. A hateful person does this, and for no reason I might add.

Behind this surface level, behind this cover story, it was being done for the agent in charge of this Mobbing who I call The Clown. It was her idea. And again this says something about HER. Now again as we look at the real level, the agent level, who does this because they were asked to? Either a nasty, disgusting, hateful, person in the first place who did it because they could care less, or someone who has been convinced to, under false pretense because of lies and manipulating in regards to that person. Now these agents can also claim "It was one of our agents", and maybe it was- but job-title does not work here as an excuse, it is still nasty and disgusting and says something about the kind of person involved. In fact this whole thing does- it says something about the Clown. She decided to target my kid, a two year old, and did so to get to me. It is SICK, not a matter of being professional, and it is extremely personal on her end as well. It says something about the psychology of the person calling the shots. That said the Clown is a psychopath and our lives are full of events which prove this, one more thing agencies did not bother finding out.

Now let's look at this from normal life. What is a normal reaction to this behavior? Minus shock most parents would be angry at the person who did this; this is more than an issue of violating social norms it is disturbing and it is sick.

Well after this, this began to escalate and to happen more and more until my kid and I were both constantly and continuously attacked when we went outside. This became constantly reoccurring. Like anyone when this is going on you begin looking out for your kid. And I might point out here we are no longer talking about normal life here as the context of normal life does not even exist anymore when it is happening all of the time. It reached a point of, "If we go out we will have problems". The public began doing this all of the time, each person only looking at their own small part unaware of how much this was actually going on in my life and my kids life. That is because they were compartmentalized, being told only enough to do what they were told to do- not told the real reason for doing so. If people had understood HOW MUCH this was going on they might not have taken part, as they would have understood a few things. They would have understood they were being used, lied to, and manipulated to do something nasty and for very nasty reasons. The amount of times that this was happening would have convinced some that there was something wrong with the picture.

So I became watchful which is understandable given the circumstances. There is not a parent on the planet who would not have been. Now on this point the Spooks claimed I was "paranoid and sensitive"- it is an obvious lie and apparently they were already claiming this. This was the sales pitch to the public which they sold before the events occurred. They told the public that I was overly sensitive in regards to my kid which again given CONTEXT was a lie and manipulation on the agents end. They just did not give the people context, they did not give the truth, proper context so that people could make an informed decision. So the public believed that they were helping out with a sensitivity problem when in reality they were being used and misused to create that very problem. They in fact were being used to create and condition the very problem they had been told I had in the first place, which was a lie. These citizens are non-questioning fools and were so because of a badge and job-title.

Until the Clown started all of this there never was a problem. And she made these citizens look like idiots by using them to try and create and condition a problem that was not there in the first place, and used and misused them to try and create the problem she said I already had. They were brainless, non-questioning, and stupid. None of these people even considered how much this was happening to me and my kid. None of them even tried considering what this would be like if it were them and their kid. Nobody looked at the REALITY of any of this. When reality goes out the window it stinks of programming, look at the viewpoint they had and their actions based on this. It stinks of cult and brainwashing because it is, the psychology is exactly the same and government is using this. And as time went on of course I was looking, and as my kid was singled out and attacked of course I had a problem- no parent would not. But these citizens were told I had a sensitivity problem and so they saw things this way, not as things really were, not reality. The context had been removed, hidden.

This is called programming and it turns people into absolute robots. The people were told to see what they were programmed to see. Their perceptions had been altered so that they saw and experienced things differently than how they really were. They were wearing false perceptions because they had believed that what they were told was true. This is a way of controlling people, of manipulating them for control of their minds. It is a form of subtle brainwashing as the people are programmed like a computer program, functioning as they have been programmed to, and it starts by telling lies and explaining actions and experiences in advance with lies. You are given "sunglasses to wear", and everything is seen through these and experienced through these and it is all incorrect.

Thus they ask people to do something and based on knowing what they are doing to me and my kid these agents of course can predict the outcome and reactions based on this. In other words they know what my kid and I will be like based on all of the facts and the real level, reality, the reality which is going on which they have not shared with the public. They know that how my kid and I are in this weird situation is actually not reacting differently than anyone else given the circumstances. In other words given this weird context, the psychology involved on my kid's end and mine was normal and predictable. And based on this the agents prepare citizens with lies, explaining our behavior before it has occurred so that they do not see it as it really is. The people are whitewashed with lies before so that they see things differently later, than they really are.

My reactions and my kid's had already been explained and in a way which was deceitful, before these citizens got involved for particular events and circumstances: Staged-Events.

Many people became convinced of something not true, and became more convinced after taking part in helping the agents and "seeing and experiencing these things". They were not even seeing and experiencing things correctly, they were merely experiencing things as they were told to, as they were told things were. In reality it was all a lie, deceit, and manipulation. They had their "programming sunglasses" on.

These government agents get away with this and everyone believes them because of a badge, blind respect for authority, and a job-title. It is ridiculously easy for these agents and people with half a brain should realize that agents asking them to break the laws and to do illegal things can not be good people. As a point, a few years later they had someone masturbate at the public library when I was there with my kid and while one of these agents stood by laughing about it and making direct eye contact with me just to let me know it was them- these agents. Good people? How do you think one of these people from Stalking would feel if it was them and their child instead? Think that at that point they might get the correct perspective? Our rights are their rights and strangely enough people involved in this Stalking do not get this.

The idea of normal life got thrown out the window from the beginning. When you know based on many experiences that you and your kid are going to be singled out and attacked, then this IS reality. It is not a matter of it all being in my head or "sensitivity", this happened every time we went outside and I knew it would be this way- so did my kid, a two year old. The context is not "real life" at that point, but it is reality. These dumb citizens however were not told this and quite obviously never thought deep enough to even figure a few things out- because of a badge. It sounds like the psychology involved in fascist movements and the Stanford Prison Experiment because it is. People did not think or care about what they were doing, they only cared about obeying authority, it is weird and kooky, it is cult. Context was hidden and deliberately removed so they did not know the truth of the matter. Otherwise they would not have gone along with these agents. How hard is this to get?

They were told to do this and told "real life" was that me and my kid were simply sensitive. The citizens and I and my kid were on two different levels and only I, my kid, and these agents knew the real level, which is REALITY. These citizens were told what to see, given a deliberately inaccurate psychological profile which could explain the behavior, but which was false. My psychology and actions as a result were different than they perceived. My psychology and my kid's was based on reality not lies and manipulations. Pieces of reality, context, had been removed. A false profile about me created as a center piece for selling a false viewpoint to citizens, who in turn became False-Witnesses.

They were told and given a viewpoint to wear in order to benefit these agents; which is the point of doing this in the first place It was a deliberate re-writing of events to convince people of a profile not mine, to give these citizens a "cause" and justification which is what is needed for fascist movements in the first place: in order to get people to take part in one. For them "Seeing was believing" except in the case of programming it is not. This is also why people in Stalking are told to not ask questions and told to not listen as these agents do not want people having all of the context.

Again this is why this psychology is illegal and why cults and extremist movements are watched closely. Yet look at who is doing this here-government agents. And in this case they were lying to and manipulating the public to get them to attack an innocent man and his child. And in ways that they would not like either. If this is not cult then what is it? If this is not a movement and Wave then what is it? If this is not brainwashing and the actions of brainwashed people then what is it?

It is conspiracy, it is illegal, and it is disgusting. And your tax dollars and government are responsible for this. Think that any of this has to do with protecting the people and terrorism? Do my daughter and I look protected here? Of course not but it does have to do with illegal laws and programs. Does anyone know of this stuff? If you look at television you would never know. Looking at a computer is another story, but then they will be reformatting the Internet soon so that it is as worthless and informative as television, so if you are going to look this material up and research I recommend that you start now. Again I have a chapter on this Internet reformatting so back to programming the public.

The public did not see and experience things as I, my kid and these agents did. How could they, they were totally confused about what reality was, they were False Witnesses. They were ignorant dupes telling themselves that they were seeing things from a real life perspective in their minds, when in fact they were not. And to top it off once these citizens experienced these events with these false perceptions, it became burned in their minds this way, it became engrained this way in their minds. The event as they experience it incorrectly only serves to reinforce their mis-perceptions: they are deaf, dumb, and blind. They became FALSE WITNESSES and the agents became airtight in any argument to the contrary (Truth). THE CITIZENS DID NOT EXPERIENCE THINGS AS THEY ACTUALLY WERE- thus they were False Witnesses, convinced of what they saw and experienced without actually knowing the truth of the matter. This is how I was framed and framed repeatedly. It is sick and people practicing this psychology regardless of job-title and badges, and just like any cult leader, belong in jail. This illegal misuse of psychology by government agents needs to be exposed.

Let's look at it clearly and truthfully.

The only ones not acting normal were the citizens and these citizens furthermore were doing things they would normally not do to someone, and to top it off they would not do these things to anyone for these reasons in the first place. Never mind TO A KID. In other words in real life, for the reasons given, they would not do this to anyone in the first place. Their behavior here clearly points to them being brainwashed which is all programming is, it is just more subtle. It also points to a blind and stupid faith in authority- they had become like robots. This is the Truth of the matter but these citizens can no longer see this. They are convinced and believe that they are justified and entitled because of "authority and a badge", they felt justified in what they were doing even though they clearly were not. All of it like the Stanford Prison Experiment, it is just like any study on Fascism and Waves. How is that for screwed up? THIS is programming and it is being misused in these government programs.

People literally let someone else control their thinking and actions, based on their perceptions being controlled and blind respect for authority. Once these agents start controlling your perceptions you can forget it, this is where programming starts. And in Mobbing this is always done to the people closest to the target FIRST, because these people are the biggest threat to possibly exposing these agents and this program, therefore they have to be the most controlled.

Over time once the citizens have been in contact with agents long enough, the citizens simply take things for granted and believe everything they are told without even questioning it- blind faith. Eventually the programming process becomes complete and like an infected computer program citizens accept things without question, they become brainless robots- the Borg (to use a Star Trek term). Once they do they are manipulated more heavily, and in the case of the Clown who is extremely corrupt, they are absolutely misused. And this says something about the Clown, about her personality, and it says something about the type of person she is. In fact this whole scenario I have just explained does. As I have come to realize this program of Stalking attracts corrupt agents as you have to be sick to be doing any of this in the first place.

To give you an idea, this extreme behavior of the public became so prevalent it reached a point where my kid at the age of two could tell that we were about to have a problem with someone and would stick her tongue out at them (And my kid was accurate). Think about this, think about how much this must have been going on. And keep in mind that this is all the result of me knowing about two cover-ups in regards to a pedophile police officer and racist murderer from twenty years ago: for this my family is attacked and traumatized. Does any of it make sense? Of course not.

In fact for many people this is a major sticking point, people all want to somehow believe that there must be a "better reason", a logical cause, which makes sense out of all of it- there is not. Framings are framings and you would think that the average citizen would ask why I would be followed and harassed for twenty years without actually being arrested, and at the cost of at least twenty million dollars, yet they do not. They are pathetic fools getting their hands filthy for corrupt agents and a corrupt government program, while throwing away their freedoms, and all because of a pedophile cop and racist in health services.

How much dumber can it get right? Actually in my case it gets even more ridiculous and stupid as this agent the Clown is actually killing some of the citizens of this country because she is sick, and now agencies have been tricked to the point of thinking I am Lex Luthor. They have let a gang of killers go free and I get the blame, typical. Maybe I will buy a cape and costume, on the other hand money and a lawyer or firm will straighten this all out. In the meantime keep an eye open for me on You Tube or elsewhere as I will obviously have to start making this more public simply based on the shoes I and my family wear- for protection, a public spot light because agencies of this land have not done their jobs. Like I have a choice.

So if you are paying attention this is how programming works within Mobbing and within COINTELPRO. For all intents and purposes Mobbing is simply when COINTELPRO steps out of the shadows and is made deliberately obvious to the target, and again they both use programming.

A SUMMARY OF PROGRAMMING

So this is how programming works below.

They plan events ahead of time. These are called by me Staged-Events.

They tell people how the target will think, feel, react to the Staged-Event. They are given "programming sunglasses" to wear.

The target's reality dictates how the target will think, feel, react; the reality is this Mobbing and what is going on within it.

The citizens from the beginning are not given all of the information, CONTEXT IS REMOVED and information is hidden. They are not given the target's real perspective or all of the facts. They are not given reality, reality is hidden.

The citizens are given a False-Viewpoint of the target, they are given a FALSE PROFILE of the target. And then they are lied to based on this.

From this False Perspective and a False Profile of the target that is sold to the citizens, the citizens are prepared and pre-lied to- whitewashed in regards to the Staged-Event. They are told "The target will react this way because of this", or "Because he is sensitive", or whatever fits the False-Profile. The possible and most likely reactions are explained to the citizens from a viewpoint of the target that is FALSE. And the funny thing is these agents are able to predict your reactions based on knowing what all of the facts are, based on reality: based on what they are going to do to you. Thus when the citizens see and experience the Staged-Event with the target, they in fact do not have a clear picture of what is going on with the target and therefore do not have a clear idea of what they are seeing and experiencing. They become False-Witnesses.

The citizens think they know what they are seeing, they think they know what they are experiencing, they think they know why things are the way they are, they think they know what the deal is with the target, they think they know the perspective of the target, they think they know why the target "reacts or acts" the way that they do within the Staged-Event, and the final irony is they "think, see, and experience this" based on being lied to and manipulated. They do not think at all on their own, they do not even begin to do any "thinking".

Which is the point, this is about being tricked into letting other people do your thinking, and from there controlling your actions: it is brainwashing. The reality is they are not thinking on their own, they are "thinking, seeing, experiencing" based on how they were TOLD TO. They are not thinking on their own or taking and making actions on their own. Common sense, reason, and the word "normal" go right out the window. Does it look like they are acting normal? They look like cult and act like cult because the same process is being used on them, and just like with cults they are being misused for someone else's purposes which are not good.

They haven't a clue as to what "normal" is at that point. And it is looking at the bigger picture that points to this, and that points to reality, yet they do not see this. It should be obvious that they have been brainwashed. What else to call it? And normal here is: they would normally not be doing this to someone in real life.

This is dangerous behavior on the part of government, I would say unprecedented behavior, but when you look at the public exposure of MK-Ultra and COINTELPRO it should be obvious that it is not. Not only is this not unprecedented but this Mobbing does in fact involve BOTH Mk-Ultra and COINTELPRO, it also involves the same psychology as the Stanford Prison Experiment. It should be obvious that government has continued with it's pursuit of these programs regardless, and that if these programs were illegal then, then they are STILL ILLEGAL now regardless of a name change. It is all still illegal and dangerous and it is a total misuse of the citizens and public.

That is the point of programming. To get people to do things, say things, see things, believe things, they normally would not, in order to affect and attack the target, to destroy the mental health of the target, to do what the agents want them to do. It is all about TORTURING the target by misusing people to inflict traumas. It is a clear example of brainwashing and cult, the public sees everything with blinders on. Programming is standard operational procedure for government agents and these illegal programs, it is also ugly and disgusting if you are me, my kid, and my girlfriend.

AN END TO THIS CHAPTER

So for my readers the piece above is on programming and gives a good idea of how nasty Mobbing and COINTELPRO are. I hope this is a help for others as this programming is nasty business and as knowing how it works can go a long ways to exposing it and neutralizing it. If you pay attention you can even see this misused in the news, a lot of the same techniques are used for selling the public stories and for selling a viewpoint to go along with these stories which make the news. Really the news these days is about telling us what to think while at the same time avoiding all of the really important topics, issues, stories- unless you are a fan of Paris Hilton.

If you need proof ask yourself why the media has taken so long to make an issue of the economy and America's debt. Or ask yourself why has the media made an issue of cow flatulence when obviously people are the greatest polluters of the planet. Or for that matter ask yourself why the news of Mobbing and COINTELPRO has not happened yet. There are literally thousands and thousands of people across the world who are being subjected to these programs, no doubt millions of people, yet the media has done nothing and said nothing. No emphasis is being put on real issues, real issues are being avoided in the news. Now look at a situation like WikiLeaks where COINTELPRO is what is being misused against Julian Assange: the media is being misused to make a high profile example out of him. Attacking WikiLeaks is about hiding corruption, not security of the people. This guy isn't a threat to armed forces or security, he is a threat to corrupt politicians. Why isn't THIS being addressed? It is all about altering people's perceptions, it is all about programming the people and masses. I have learned this from twenty years of this Mobbing and COINTELPRO.

Think the government has it's priorities right here? It is all illegal, all an enormous waste of money, and all for what? All for corrupt individuals, it most certainly is not about morals and ethics. Look at the INSANITY of it. If this can be happening to me, then this can be happening to ANYONE. When government has so much money, time, manpower, for such an enormous injustice, then this can happen to anyone, and EVERYONE is at risk. You have to be absolutely out of your mind to not get this. When a gunman starts shooting you run for shelter, you don't stand around asking questions and contemplating justifications of the shooter. Only an idiot putting his own life at risk would do this. Instead you look at actions and react quickly to protect yourself. Well this is how people need to be in regards to these illegal programs. There is clearly something sinister and wrong with all of this and actions of government should be what tips you off here. Waiting to be shot is the dumbest solution and accomplishes nothing. Everyone needs to wake up and become informed about these programs, these programs need to be exposed and brought out into the open as the intentions of these programs clearly is not for the greater good.

Can anyone call this protecting the people?

What is the answer then? You decide but keep in mind that my rights are your rights and that if I have none then it is only a small step in regards to you. If I have no rights then you have no rights, if my family has no rights then your family has no rights, if I and my family are attacked heavily then this can happen to you and your family. That is the answer in regards to these programs of COINTELPRO and Gang Stalking.

The answer is "WHAT IF IT WAS ME?". These programs give the power to do this to anyone, that is the point and example of my life here. There is nothing protecting you and your family anymore than there is for me and my own. Your answer and response based on this is the correct answer, quite obviously no one has any business conducting such illegal programs and most certainly not government. Look at my situation here, people have got to speak out and get active to end this all, otherwise it will shortly be "We the government", instead of "We the people". I would already know, this is what I am already dealing with: and shortly down the road, it will be what everyone is dealing with. This is what happens when people are not self-thinking and self-empowered, merely waiting for someone else to do their thinking for them.

CHAPTER 12
GREY-LAWS AND GREY PROGRAMS- LAWS DELIBERATELY
WRITTEN WITH DOUBLE MEANING FOR MISUSE: ILLEGAL-LAWS
AND PROGRAMS CREATED BY CORRUPT PEOPLE : THE PATRIOT
ACT, STALKING, COINTELPRO

The Patriot Act is named after the very people it targets. These are
what I call illegal laws, "grey laws" and grey government programs because
the real intentions are hidden in an area of grey; these laws do not even begin
to be a matter of black and white. If the real intentions of these laws and
programs are hidden then we are talking about corruption here, we are talking
about hiding things because the people will object. Why would people object?
Because they would recognize that these laws and programs are corrupt and
dangerous along with the people who came up with them. This applies to many
of the people who are active in these illegal programs as well.

As a point the government agents I deal with in my life communicated
to me, "The Constitution is only a piece of paper with ink on it.", I countered
back with "Well so are the 'laws' you claim to be following.". They do what
they do because they want to do it (violate people), and like doing it, they are
corrupt as people and not because of laws.

There is something wrong with the government when it's employees
claim the Constitution is worthless paper, and see the Constitution as an
obstacle only. Patriots are those who believe in the Constitution and America as
it is meant to be and are therefore an obstacle to very corrupt and powerful
people in government: the Elite, those who think they are above the laws and
people of America. If you want total power and total control then ideals like
freedom and democracy and people who believe in these ideals, are an obstacle
and in the way: therefore so is our Constitution.

You can not have corrupt people in government who want all of the
power, but then expect them to leave power in the hands of the people, which
you may note is what any democracy is about. Democracy is the distribution of
power amongst the masses and people, yet corrupt people who want all of the
power, want all of the power centralized at the top of government and out of
the hands of the people. These systems are commonly called dictatorships and
police-states, and many times dictatorships arise out of freedom oriented
systems because of corruption. Of course dictatorships target people who are
outspoken, independent, and who think for themselves- they target people who
see what is wrong with the system and who are critical of it. Well this is what
has happened to America. Take a look it is unmistakable. The Patriot Act and
many other things point to this.

The Patriot Act is another name for COINTELPRO, it is a renamed
version of it so that people do not recognize it for what it is. It gives total
power to do anything behind people's backs, and under false pretenses it gives

the power to investigate and interfere with anyone's life. If you substitute the word patriot for terrorist then you start to get an idea here. It is for misuse, it is corrupt, and it is for putting people in my situation of Mobbing unless I am mistaken- and I do not think that I am. In fact it points to this, and this is what I have experienced. The Patriot Act IS COINTELPRO, and COINTELPRO is just a name for a government program which creates a fascist movement behind your back in which everyone secretly cooperates with government agents and takes part in "helping them". The Patriot Act brings COINTELPRO one step closer to being accepted and out in the open.

Now when you look at the wording of the Patriot Act and substitute the word patriot for terrorist you see that this can all easily be about patriots and your average citizen. It most certainly is "grey" and again the specific wording has been chosen for deliberate misuse. It has been worded in such a way as to make it acceptable, when in fact it is deliberately written so that it can be misused on the public and citizens in secret. It is misdirection.

Terrorism is the cover story, it is all about targeting patriots and citizens, and the reasons for being on this "list of suspects" I guarantee you are not good ones. This explains why there are so many names on the No Fly List, and why the government has denied this- keep in mind that the No Fly List until 9/11 had less than twenty names on it. My own circumstances here say a lot about this. No, these terrorists we keep hearing about are actually citizens who believe in right and wrong, and who believe in ideals and their country- again patriots. In the future these terrorists are going to be anyone who does not go along with corrupt government once an economy crash happens. It can be looked at as a statement of the future they have prepared for when patriots become the enemy and "terrorists".

The government will declare martial law and anyone not going along with government at that point will be branded a radical and terrorist- as defined by the Patriot Act. In my opinion the Patriot Act was written with this economy crash in mind, and certainly for some world trauma which causes an uproar. And thanks to this government program of Stalking, government will already have a Citizen Spy Network in place for rounding anyone up that is not faithful to corrupt government and corrupt politicians- once the economy crashes. All of this is about power.

Those not agreeing with martial law will be declared the enemies, and will be sought out by Obama's Citizen Police Force. This Stalking has been all about creating the groundwork for a small army of sell-outs and snitches, those who will do anything for government, and creating the infrastructure and connections needed. It is all about thinking ahead, it is all about corrupt politicians and their corrupt friends preparing ahead for an economy crash.

Now let's look together at many of the things these corrupt politicians are doing, which point to the misuse of the Patriot Act, and which point to the preparation for an economy crash and martial law.

We have COINTELPRO and Stalking which are about creating a fascist wave. Again just like citizens of Germany during the time of Hitler's rise to power they are blind and the groundwork and foundation for a police-state is being created with them. The citizens involved think that this can't be true, that they could not make the same mistakes, yet they are. The government has already studied how fascism all works, the psychology of it, and has perfected it since the times of Hitler and the Red Scare. Citizens spying on other citizens and attacking other citizens is not about democracy, quite the obvious, yet they remain ignorant and clueless. They are in fact an insult to America and real Americans. Stalking is about creating blind respect for authority, it is about more power and control for government, it is NOT about protecting people.

Then you have a No Fly List which stinks of Old Soviet Style monitoring and controlling of citizens movements because that is what it is, the only difference being that now it is America doing it. Again a warning sign and a measure taken from a police state (the USSR).

Then you have Guantanamo Bay in which torture prisons have been set up, the people within them have not even had a day in court, and clearly this is not justice or democracy. But it is a warning sign: their rights are your rights, and they have none. Guantanamo Bay is simply to profile the public, and to desensitize the public to the torture and atrocities being committed there, along with being held captive without even having a trial. Kind of the way it was when German citizens were living next to prison camps during Nazi Germany...

Now to add to all of this we have what the government calls Custodial Facilities all across America, and capable of holding MILLIONS of people. In the meantime if you are on the No Fly List you may want to start wondering if Custodial Facilities are going to be like Guantanamo Bay... Again a clear warning sign but since the government says Custodial Facilities are for "The Great Mexican Invasion" (I heard this on public radio) then it must be so- an instant flood and invasion from Mexico which the government never gave a reason for. Of course Mexicans no doubt all plan on doing this collectively after the dollar crashes and becomes worthless, if you get my point.

Then you have the Patriot Act which is deliberately written for misuse, and which is actually about targeting patriots. It is in fact COINTELPRO under a different name so that it is acceptable, and sold under false pretenses to get people to accept it- like the Red Scare. Again more signs. To add to all of this, there are obviously plans for shutting down and reformatting the Internet in 2012 as well, and this is a major sign and tell that there are plans in place for 2012 by these corrupt Elite (possibly early 2013). Shutting down the Internet and reformatting it is all about eliminating communications so that the people have less information and power, and then returning the Internet after strict controls and measures have been put in place. The Internet will be totally controlled the way it is in police state countries except this will be worldwide.

The pieces are all there. They plan on doing something or multiple things for centralizing all power, and based on the signs this is about a police state, a dictatorship being set up. Once you look at what they plan on doing to the economy then you realize that at the best it will be socialism which is sold to us and just underneath that a dictatorship. In fact the socialism will only be a thin veil and cover story for a fascist government and a world government at that if their plans succeed. That is what these Grey Laws, Acts, and programs are about.

If you are looking and paying attention this will all most likely start over an economy crash and then snowball from there. An economy crash is just around the corner regardless of talk, there are economic realities that have to be looked at here. This Gang Stalking, the Patriot Act, the No Fly List, Custodial Facilities, the Internet shutdown and reformatting, it is all about politicians keeping their power after the economy crashes, and it is all about turning everyone else into criminals instead- it is all reversed. Look at all of the signs and points I have just listed, it is unmistakable, and a lot of this involves these Grey Laws and programs, as I call them.

A SUMMARY AND END TO THIS CHAPTER

This Terrorism Scare is the Red Scare all over again and is what has resulted in the Patriot Act. That is what all of this is about all of it. It is about taking all rights away from the public, it is about making the tactics of police states, COINTELPRO, legal.

Americans have not changed overnight suddenly becoming a threat to the American people, the government has. The government is targeting patriots not terrorists. It is about targeting patriots and an assortment of others who corrupt government agents decide are to be attacked and targeted by government. It is disgusting and is about laying down the groundwork for fascism. Programming is used by cults and now it is being used by government on it's own people and all across the world in many lands. Again fascism is when government becomes cult, and fascism is evil by nature and created by dangerous psychopaths in the first place.

It is no longer "We the People", but "We the Government".

The Patriot Act under emotional circumstances, and therefore people were not thinking clearly and thus easily manipulated, was passed for the wrong reasons. It should have been well thought out, well scrutinized by the people, not hurried and hidden by corrupt politicians. Which is why it was passed when it was. When you look at the Patriot Act you realize that ANYONE can be a suspect, anyone with an opposing viewpoint, anyone critical of corrupt government. Strangely enough it can be misused to target people who are out-spoken and critical of government; it gives authority to government to spy and take away the freedoms of anyone who has a viewpoint which is critical of the government. This is democracy? This is a farce.

And as corrupt as government is these days, people are going to trust government with these laws and programs? Has everyone lost their minds?! That is rather the point, you can be investigated for simply criticizing government- and that does not even begin to be about democracy. This is not simply happening to some far away people in a movie, it is happening to millions of people across the world, these laws, Acts, and programs are already being misused and used in criminal ways- my life is proof of this. This all resembles the Red Scare because it is. In the meantime as government goes about violating peoples' rights it denies that it is doing so, which is ridiculous. It has written these laws and created these programs for that very purpose. Look at all of the people on the Internet being violated by these corrupt laws and programs, it is about nothing but the violation of people's rights and conspiracy. You are expecting corrupt politicians to clean up corruption within government?

People had better wake up to the reality of these Grey Laws and programs and had better realize that these Grey Laws are actually a tactic. A tactic for creating laws which are to be deliberately misused. If you believe the Patriot Act is not being misused then you had better take another look.

How blind can Americans be? And others in their lands where this is happening as well? This is the world you live in not the one you want to live in. Until we as people decide to be responsible and self-empowered, become proud again of our heritage, our country (countries) will continue to go downhill, and corrupt politicians will continue to encroach on our rights as a people. Our land and lands will continue to be reverse engineered until there is nothing left but the worst of possibilities and options, IF people do nothing.

People have got to put the Constitution, freedom, and "doing the right thing" first. As things are now these corrupt politicians have become so fat and powerful they are now targeting an entire portion of the population who are a threat to their corrupt lifestyle.

Patriots are the first people to speak out and institute change in regards to a corrupt government and corrupt politicians because of the Love for their country. Patriots are the FIRST ONES to protect their country. How blind can anyone be? This is what this Patriot Act is about, other people's self-interests and it is being sold as "patriotic". There is nothing patriotic about it. Other programs like Stalking exist for the same reasons, for targeting patriots, and this has been agreed to internationally- you are hearing this directly from someone who would know. I speak from experience here, in terms of information it does not get better than this.

In fact I, and now my family, continue to be targeted and in ways that even agencies would not agree with. All of this corruption is spreading like a DISEASE and a mental disease at that. NOW this is happening to me and my family, LATER it could be you and your own. When it is other people and their families, then people will start caring about what I write of here. After all at that point you will know it is true when it happens to you.

My life and now my families is the result of corrupt politicians, corrupt agents, and corrupt programs. In fact currently as I prepare information for another agency of this country, I am receiving death threats all over again. The agent in charge, the Clown, has totally lied to and manipulated two agencies and has tricked them into not investigating: and it is as simple as asking my witnesses questions. Naturally now that they have gotten away with a cover-up they feel confident in getting away with killing me, once things have settled down. And I told these agencies what is going on yet they have NOT looked: and I have documentation, witnesses, notes, observations and memories. Again with witnesses the capture of these agents is guaranteed but agencies have been tricked and suckered. It is all one big corrupt mess, it is all the result of corrupt programs created by corrupt politicians and subservient fools at agencies who rather believe in a job-title first rather than find out what is going on.

At least for some people you may feel protected by the Patriot Act and other pieces of legislation, I and my family do NOT. You may believe in a job title that says nothing about the person doing the job, we do not. You may believe blindly in a badge, we do not. We are already experiencing the reality of government and these programs which the government has to hide to avoid getting in trouble. We are quite clear about who the "terrorists" are here and they have government badges. If you need proof that agencies and governments do not begin to be about protecting the people then this would be it. I have a child and family with two dead pets because of government agents and government programs. THAT is the reality of these corrupt programs and laws, and THAT is the result of at least 20 million dollars being spent. A lot of pain and suffering, two dead pets, for a minimum of 20 million of your tax dollars, and to keep a pedophile and murdering racist out of jail. And this all can easily fall into the category of the Patriot Act in multiple ways.

Justice?

The Patriot Act, COINTELPRO, Stalking, all of these grey laws and grey programs are about corrupt politicians who want more power and control. There is something wrong with politicians when they write such laws and programs in the first place, they know this or else they would not be hiding it all from the mainstream media. The Terrorism Scare is just like the Red Scare all over again for a reason. If you look at the Red Scare you will see that the real enemy was the government, and all of the "paranoia" was about greater control. And if you look at the Terrorism Scare you will see that it is the same way all over again: people around the world have got to start waking up and waking up quickly. If Americans and people of other lands do not wake up soon it will only be "We the government" instead of "We the people"- as it is the people are already being divided. If you look it is already happening, I and my family would know.

CHAPTER 13
THE TERRORISM-SCARE EQUALS THE RED-SCARE OUR CONSTITUTION TRAMPLED BY SECRET AND ILLEGAL LAWS AND PROGRAMS

This Mobbing I am in, COINTELPRO, and the Patriot Act are I believe about a plan for a grim future, in which many world events begin happening. A future planned for New World Order. For the sake of this chapter I will focus on Stalking/Mobbing as it is what I know best. It is an illegal program that is a product of illegal laws. If you do not want to believe that last statement, knock yourself out, but it sure is not about democracy. And if you look on the Internet this Mobbing, is prevalent across the world and seems to be growing in volume which points to a world conspiracy, which clearly points to multiple governments being involved and in mutual agreement about these programs. This started in America, followed me to Asia, and now to Europe, so my life rather settles this issue. More people are being targeted all around the world, and these days terrorists and terrorism are the false pretense for investigating harmless citizens: good people who care about the state of things with an opinion or viewpoint contrary to corrupt government. More illegal laws and programs have been created for getting people targeted by COINTELPRO and in this Mobbing: because of corrupt politicians not terrorism. All of this fanaticism and paranoia has been orchestrated by corrupt politicians for their own good, not ours. The system and government are becoming more fanatical and taking all of our rights in the name of terrorism; it is the Red Scare all over again, look at all of the similarities, it is scary and amazing.

In reality this is not about terrorism, this Terrorism Scare like the Red Scare is about manipulating people emotionally, through fear, for greater control. Corrupt politicians are the ones who have written and passed these illegal laws, implementing illegal programs like COINTELPRO and Stalking, to protect their power-base and self-interests as they prepare to implement plans in 2012 and or early 2013. These laws and programs give government the power to investigate and interfere with anyone and you have no rights or options: they want that they can monitor, interfere, and investigate anyone. This is a sign of a government preparing for a police-state. It is fanatical. Like this COINTELPRO and Mobbing situation I am in. This Terrorism Scare has been used as an excuse for creating corrupt programs and laws which target individuals and gets the public's hands dirty on behalf of corrupt government. It is all very much like the Red Scare and I see very little difference. The ONLY difference I see is that this time government is being much more careful, subtle, and invisible, to make sure that it's encroachment on our rights is not detected and exposed for being as bad and severe as it is. The government has learned and perfected it's methods since the Red Scare.

These corrupt politicians and their Elite friends heading corporations and companies, are going after citizens who are in the way. They are preparing the way for their next step, a world economic crash, and New World Order. They are designing and creating a population which attacks others within it, who are against what corrupt government says or does. In this way they are training the population to conform to government and to attack those who are critical of it and to attack those who are for POSITIVE CHANGE. In essence those citizens without a brain are being trained to attack those who are capable of thinking for themselves. There are those who do as they are told attacking those who "do and think on their own". You have those who do not think for themselves, those without self-empowerment, attacking those who practice independent thought and thinking, those who think for themselves, those who are self-empowered. You have people who make up their own mind being attacked by people who let the television do it for them. Which is what television is really about, it is about telling us what to fixate on, telling us what is important subject wise, and it is about telling us what to think in regards to particular subjects. The media and news have sunken and fallen.

What you have are a bunch of citizens being trained to defend the corrupt who are making a mess of the world in the first place, and they are being trained to attack the very people who would fix this world. It has gone from corrupt politicians who have created corrupt programs which attracts corrupt agents, to ignorant citizens who are used for violating the rights of others: and based on what they do not know. These ignorant citizens get used to enforce a corrupt system. In my case in particular I was put in this Mobbing because I knew of a pedophile police officer, and a racist and murder, and I knew of the two resulting cover-ups. COINTELPRO got involved because of this, framed me, and put me in this Mobbing which none of these citizens knew, or knows about: Again this Mobbing and Gang Stalking is the next level of COINTELPRO. They simply believed everything they were told and supported very corrupt agents who were supporting a pedophile cop and a murdering racist in health services. THIS is what these grey laws and illegal programs are for, and this is what this Terrorism Scare is for: for greater control. People have lost their minds. Just as these framings about me are sold to manipulate people into helping these agents, so it is that the public is being scared into going along with this Terrorism Scare. Out of fear they are being manipulated.

Only an imbecile and fool does not see this as illegal in America (stuff like this is only legal in police-states), and only a fool does not see this as preparation for a new government system- closet fascism. Only an imbecile does not see these illegal laws and programs that are being implemented, as the creation and implementation of fascism. COINTELPRO, this Mobbing, and laws like the Patriot Act, are NOT about American ideals or democracy, they are a violation of this. This is about democratic ideals is it? This is about and because of terrorism is it?

When terrorists have already changed and transformed a democracy into a nation of fear, borrowing tactics and measures from a police-state, then terrorists have already won. This is when the ideals of America and democracy should be raised as a standard bearer, the constitution raised as our flag and defiance be given to any that would seek to damage or maim our country by changing our country from within (like corrupt politicians), and getting us to trample our constitution, freedom, rights, and ideals out of fear. THIS is what being an American is about. This is when being an American counts the most- those willing to give up our Constitution, rights, ideals, and freedom for "terrorists" can kiss my patriot ass. Are you an American, or are you more afraid of terrorists? DON'T TREAD ON ME.

Patriots all across the world have got to stand up for their countries and oppose those who would destroy them. I am not one to normally think in these kinds of terms but it is all really a matter of evil vs. good, there is no better description. Again this is why you see me refer to the Harry Potter books at times within this book, because this is a perfect comparison.

As far as I am concerned this talk of terrorists separates real Americans from wannabee Americans. People who are absolute buffoons willing to throw away the Constitution, the HEART AND SOUL of our country, people who are willing to let what makes us American be thrown out, people who are willing to let the Constitution be trampled for terrorists, for complete losers. Where are your heads? You are an American? As far as I am concerned you only live in America. The requirements are greater than simply living in America and saying you are an American, you actually have to be one. It doesn't take anything to say that you are one. You can not throw out the heart and soul of our country, change it into something lesser and claim to believe in America: you can not throw out what makes us America and then claim to be an American. Saying you are an American is one thing, being one requires more. Being a patriot means loving your country and fighting for it's preservation, it does NOT mean throwing out the heart and soul of your country and fighting for corrupt politicians.

All of this fear mongering, which is exactly what it is, all done in the name of terrorists, is out of control. Terrorists are fanatics and extremists willing to do anything for their cause and now government is acting the same way. Now government is controlling people, the public, out of fear and has the people acting the same way. It is hysteria and fear and it is being misused to eat up the country from the inside. Non-thinking citizens are not only allowing this to happen but as evidenced by my situation of this Mobbing, they are helping this to happen. All of this resembles, AND IS, the Red Scare all over again. Now the public is acting fanatical as well and in regards to itself. Coincidence?

Now illegal laws and programs are being implemented wide scale which target Americans. Out of fear and fear mongering the people have become the enemy. And now government is being put on a pedestal. It is like "The War on Drugs" which was a flop. It is all misdirection and divide and conquer of the people. And now COINTELPRO and my Mobbing are being used and misused to implement this, to put government on a pedestal and to make sure it is no longer "We the People", but "We the Government". The shell of democracy remains while the inside has been eaten away and destroyed for a bunch of criminals, corrupt politicians, in the name of "terrorists".

This IS the Red Scare all over again. This time period we live in now, in the future when looking back on history, will be labeled the Terrorism Scare. And until people reclaim their brains- which they have lost because of a single large trauma from the Twin Towers and 9/11, we will continue to de-evolve as a country and as Americans. America is running backwards and in reverse because of it, America is being reverse engineered because of it. The heart and soul of America, the Constitution, is being over- run by corrupt government and people have virtually lost all of their rights. My rights are your rights and I have none. Behind your back the government now has the right to do anything it wants in regards to your life: it never used to be this way or so bad. The Twin Towers, 9/11, was a trauma induced and misused to manipulate the people and masses, MK-Ultra on a Global-Scale. The Terrorism Scare IS the Red Scare all over again.

CHAPTER 14
THE PATH OF EXPERIENCE VS. THE PATH OF CONSCIOUSNESS

You have a big hole in your roof. You have two ways of learning here: through consciousness, thinking, conscious-thought, or through experience. The conscious route involves looking at the situation clearly, realizing there is a problem, that it needs to be taken care of right away, and then doing something about it. Consciousness, self-empowerment, responsibility, and action are the formula here. If you do not do something about it then "experience" will result. Being conscious means you think, realize, and choose not to have the experience that would happen if you did nothing. You choose something different, a different course, a different route.

In my case I like the conscious route, the Path of Consciousness.

Now the other way of learning, the masses way of learning for a very long time now, the dumb way, is called the Path of Experience.

In this case you have a big hole in your roof but choose to do nothing about it, perhaps lying to yourself, "I'll get to it later", or perhaps procrastinating and deciding to do it next week, realizing you have no way of predicting the outcome of the weather until then. Or perhaps you don't really think about what can happen at all and simply ignore it for the sake of convenience and comfort: this is laziness of the mind. This is called being ignorant, and it is still a matter of making a choice. In this case what happens is that the predictable happens: it rains.

If we ignore problems they tend to get bigger until we are forced to deal with them. This is one of the ways the "Universe", the Divine, the Source, Allah, God, evolves consciousness. This is a matter of energy and what I call Human-Physics, it is really a matter of Divine-Law. In essence this is evolution- the dumb, non-thinking, non-learning, die off. This is Darwinism of Consciousness. Thus it is better for mankind to deal with problems as they come up before it is too late, before problems get so large that by the time we realize they are there (because we have been looking the other way) we are shocked by the experience. If we try to ignore a problem, however small in the beginning, it will continue to grow until it calls our attention. Unfortunately by the time it does we often times end up shocked and traumatized by the experience. All because we chose the Path of Experience, allowing the problem and it's energy to build to shocking proportions.

As the problem is ignored the energy builds, it grows and gets worse to call attention to itself. The longer you wait, the more complicated and difficult it gets to repair. This is a matter of the law of cause and effect, a universal law, a divine-law. This is a matter of balance. Thus the longer you wait the more energy is required to repair a problem. The more negative energy that builds up, the more positive energy it takes to repair a problem- again balance, the law of cause and effect.

This is what is happening in this world today, mankind is beginning to wake up and realize the mess it is in. A large segment of mankind is beginning to wake up, realize responsibility is needed, and is wanting it's own self empowerment back (thus taking it back from government and politicians) because the people see that their leaders are not actually doing their jobs. As a result of people waking up they are relying more on themselves to see the Truth of things and seeing more,, including manipulations of the Elite and the problems of our world today. Positive energy, self-empowered people, the Path of Consciousness, is beginning to respond and take effect pushing back against the insanity of corrupt politicians, the Elite, and their deliberately made problems: their reverse-engineering of humanity and the world. As corruption spreads like a disease so does self-empowerment and doing the right thing. In this case we can think of this as being white blood cells and anti-bodies, a building up of our mental immune system to that which is negative and corrupt. In one very real sense this is what I do: I try to bring up the problems with humanity so they can be dealt with before it is too late. I promote the Path of Consciousness. A good prophecy is one that does not come true. But back to my example of Mr. Laziness and rain.

Through bad decision making you have chosen a negative experience whereas with conscious intent you could have chosen responsibility, and a good experience in comparison. So you end up with a lot of water pouring into your house, you end up totally stressed out yelling and cursing while you get drenched inside of your own home running around with a bucket, like some deranged Captain Ahab bailing out your house. But of course it did not have to be that way and of course strangely enough you chose it: you chose to have this experience. You chose the Path of Experience.

Ultimately you learn not to do it this way again and learn to do what you would have done in the first place if you had chosen the conscious way. You learn to take care of the problem right away before the problem grows, you learn to take responsibility as problems appear. Or as a lot of people are- half-serious and resistant to becoming more conscious, they learn to be more conscious in regards to a similar experience, a particular set of circumstances. Like say they only learn to take the Path of Consciousness when they have a hole in their roof again... Really the conscious way involves doing all things this way, taking care of all problems consciously and actively but at least for some it is a start.

The Path of Experience is the stupid way and it makes more sense to fix problems when the minimal amount of time (which can not be replaced) and energy is needed to repair a problem. Unfortunately here on planet Earth the masses are drunken on dodo-berries and prefer experience, I however do not.

Now on my home planet I call this learning the hard way. The funny thing is once this idiot has this experience something strange happens to him. He learns, he becomes more conscious about things. The next time he has a hole in his roof he will choose to think first, choose the Path of Consciousness, not the Path of Experience, realizing that either way he will have to take care of the problem. The irony is no matter what path you choose, you will in the end choose the Path of Consciousness. If Mr. Laziness really learns he will apply this formula to all things in the future. So why even bother with the Path of Experience, it is stupid and a waste of time and energy. Lazy minded people choose the Path of Experience but in the end learn to be more conscious anyhow.

This is how thought evolves, this is how the universe evolves consciousness. It is a natural law, a divine law, built into our reality. The law of cause and effect can be found in our daily lives, it is all a part of what I call Human-Physics: people and energy, power of the mind, the law of cause and effect.

Now what if this Mr. Laziness was our neighbor or if we were an observer of this lazy minded individual with a hole in his roof. What would we do?

Why would someone want to help a person who is not interested in fixing his own house in the first place? And what is the point of doing it for him if all he does is expect someone else to do it for him and gives up his responsibility and the learning that comes with it to others? Who would and what type of person would take this guy's responsibility upon themselves and for what purpose if they did? Under those circumstances almost all normal people would not help out. It is a matter of accepting responsibility for the situation at hand and trying to remedy it yourself that counts. For most people who would help you out this is what counts. I think we all can agree on this. No one is going to simply come and fix it for you but if they see you struggling and trying, many would and will help.

Well how are we as Americans in regards to the problems of our country and in regards to problems with our government, and corruption? How are we, humanity, when it comes to fixing our own problems? The masses are dismal at fixing anything, they are non-motivated, apathetic, blind, and lazy. Are we trying to do anything and who do we expect to change things, to fix things, and why? Are we expecting corrupt politicians to fix a corrupt system? How do you think it became corrupt in the first place? How do you think they view the masses and the public? Probably as stupid and gullible don't you think? And another important point and issue is what are the motivations of those willing to fix things when we as a people are not willing to do so ourselves? Many times anyone willing to help someone too lazy to fix their own problems is going to have ulterior motives as there is little point otherwise. People like this simply see an opportunity. The corrupt know what they can get away with in regards to the public: they know that the public and the masses are lazy minded.

This is the masses, mankind's dysfunctional weakness, it's lack of self-empowerment and responsibility for itself. We the people, humanity, use this to our disadvantage in regards to electing politicians and leaders. Corruption is rampant causing ALL of the problems of our world today yet we expect corrupt politicians and governments to fix things. We throw our responsibility and self-empowerment at politicians and this is what corrupt politicians and the Elite understand and want. I have also provided an example of how this looks, this mentality, mankind's flaw, through the Path of Consciousness and the Path of Experience- how this looks from the outside-in. This Path of Experience and Consciousness is a reoccurring theme throughout this book and for a reason; it is what the masses, world, and humanity are choosing, and they consistently choose the Path of Experience.

What do you want, the world you live in or the world you want to live in? If you want the world you want to live in then you are going to have to work for it. This means self-empowerment, taking responsibility, and action. This again means working for what you want and not waiting for others to do it for you. This means being self-empowered. The Path of Consciousness is a far better option than the Path of Experience. The Path of Consciousness in numbers will lead to a New Revolution, changes for the better in our world in an intelligent way and without problems. ..

CHAPTER 15
THE NATIONAL-DEBT PART ONE: 2012/2013, NOT IF, BUT WHEN AND WHY THE AMERICAN ECONOMY WILL COLLAPSE, AND THE WORLD-ECONOMY WITH IT: A REALITY CHECK FOR EVERYONE WHO LIKES THEIR MONEY

How about a War Against Corruption?

This is very basic, simple to understand. Seeing as how this is about peoples' money I imagine that people are a lot more questioning and analytical about information such as this. That is to say I bet a lot more people are less blind when it comes to looking at information such as this because they feel motivated out of self-interest, and are therefore less lazy minded when it comes to looking at facts. People are more realistic, observant, logical, deductive, and more reasoning, as a general rule, when it comes to their money. Having said that, as a country, as a whole, it does not look that way. Quite frankly, and as I will get to, we as a people and country look like a bunch of suckers.

The question here is, what happens to a country when it can not pay the interest on the money it owes to other countries? Never mind the money it owes, but the interest owed for the money borrowed. What happens?

As a country America owes an absolutely enormous amount of money to other countries. America has the national debt, that literally grows worse and worse by the minute. It is ridiculous to think that with the way politicians and other government branches are performing and behaving, that this debt will ever be paid off. No one is taking care of it, no one is being responsible. Corruption is not only causing those who are responsible for taking care of the debt to turn a blind eye, but is in fact the cause of much of the money being used up, and disappearing- thus increasing the debt. In fact if you look, a lot of money is being stolen by corrupt government employees, corrupt politicians sharing the gains with other government employees and contractors, who hold key positions for helping this money disappear. Friends of politicians are being deliberately over-paid, and then later politicians are getting some of this money back.

America now faces a crisis that most Americans do not even know about as a result of this disappearing money and the national debt. So what is the deal? The fact of the matter is that the American economy is going to crash in the next year or two, and 2012-2013 looks like the chosen year for this. The politicians know this, how could they not? The problem is the American people do not. The American economy is going to crash and the American dollar is going to become worthless, regardless of talk of "band aides" being put on this large flesh wound. This is based on very simple economic principals. The economic problems of 2008 was merely a profiling of the masses, for an economic crash that is about to happen. A field testing and fine tuning for the governments, and in regards to the public and masses. It was a looking at how the masses will react so that governments can be better prepared for when this actually happens. If you watch the news and pay attention, this is a common tactic of government for profiling the public and masses.

We as a nation are approaching a point where the American economy and all of the money it makes in a year will not even pay for the interest owed on the national debt. The dollar will become worthless and America bankrupt. We literally will not even be able to pay for the interest, never mind the debt itself. When this happens the dollar will become worthless, the American economy will crash, the world economy will spiral out of control and then crash, there will be a lot of instantly poor people as a result, and a lot of people will be angry. Especially Americans, but many others across the world as well, as their economies will also crash. This is in the process of happening now, and will be deliberate when it does come to pass.

Now keep in mind that American politicians, the American government knows of this impending reality, and so do other politicians and governments across the world. Thus there is a mutual agreement to remain silent about this, by world governments, a conspiracy against the people of the world, against the masses. No government is actually preparing it's people for this. No one is doing or saying anything to fix this other than a lot of talk. Instead governments are preparing to fight their own people, because of their own corruption and mistakes. And one thing is for sure, when the American economy crashes and the dollar becomes worthless, the politicians will still have money, and still be rich. This is what we are paying them for?

They have invested a lot of time and money over a period of many years into Custodial Facilities across the country, the No Fly List which monitors people and their movements, illegal government programs in which citizens are trained to blindly serve government, but they have not spent any of these many years trying to fix the actual problem. These points I have just listed give power to government and are quite obviously preparation for something down the road. My belief here is that it is for an economic crash. This will serve as a catalyst for martial law, and these preparations speak of this, they are simply waiting for a reason to make it all justified, out in the open, and totally acceptable. In order to do this they need an event, an economic crash serving this purpose.

They have done more to prepare for martial law then they have for trying to fix the economy itself. In fact money keeps "disappearing" from the government, trillions of dollars, this in turn only speeds up the process. It is like someone is robbing the country blind, into debt, and an economy crash is an escape plan. This is actually my belief, as every thing points to the setting up of a police state, martial law. With martial law is total control, and if you are a corrupt politician then you need not worry this way. Otherwise if the economy crashes and there is no martial law, then you will have a lot of people screaming for your blood and jobs, and no way out. For corrupt politicians robbing the country, if government has all of the power and control then you need not worry.

Obviously they must have something prepared for all of the civil unrest this will cause. These governments know that people will be very angry.

If they are saying nothing and doing nothing, then it is something they want and actions speak louder than words here. This secret of a coming economy crash, is only a secret from the masses, not a secret from other governments. And yes of course there is talk about economic unrest as it happens in lands such as Greece for example, but no real looking at how serious this can become. There is no focus being put on the certainty of it. It may not be Greece that starts it all, but the whole system is doomed to fail based of economic realities, this is what I am speaking of here. We have got to deal with the economic realities and it is a sure thing that the European system is a mess and America is as well. It is guaranteed to happen at some point. It is just not dealt with as a certain reality that will happen, instead it is pushed away on a shelf so that when it does happen it will be a total shock. Based on actions of governments and the reality of America's debt, it is clear that this WILL HAPPEN but this reality is not being dealt with directly, and as a result the problems are not really being fixed. Actions are what count here. Like an alcoholic you can not fix the problem until it is dealt with directly, honestly, and head on, and this is not how the economy is being addressed. But back to corruption within the American government that is using up all of America's money to the point that the American economy will collapse.

As an example, on September 10, 2001 2.3 trillion dollars was said to be "missing", lost in unaccountable transactions as said by our unaccountable representatives: 2.3 trillion dollars was said to have disappeared (and that is just for ONE year), which is of course impossible. It is in the pockets of corrupt politicians, their friends with businesses, and others within government helping them to funnel the money away. One way in which this money is disappearing is that corrupt politicians are awarding contracts to friends who own companies working for government and who are being extremely overpaid; no doubt as a result of lobbying and friendship. Remind anyone of 10,000 dollars for a hammer? This money in turn gets "shared" with politicians later, it is MONEY LAUNDERING for corrupt politicians.

Money is being taken from the American people, given to others in very large amounts (deliberate over paying), and then part of it is being given to politicians who end up later working for these overpaid companies which are owned by friends of politicians. A job gets set up for them at these companies, and they get paid a large piece of the tax payers money that they gave away by overpaying. In one way, shape, or form these corrupt politicians are receiving some of this money later. It is for all intents and purposes money laundering, illegal, and everyone is cut in on the action. The American people get robbed, and this is happening yearly. Every year it is estimated that one trillion dollars disappears- and I heard this on the radio (Nov. 2010) where all can hear it. It is all corruption and it is causing the American people's money to disappear at the cost to our country, national debt, and future economy and security. At the cost to democracy and capitalism as well as they will later try to sell us socialism, and that capitalism does not work- as I will later get to. And they say that "terrorists" are the greatest threat to America and the government is targeting citizens as a result of this pathetic cover story. Take a good look. It is the ones with the most power who are misusing it, that are the greatest threat to our country and who are held the least accountable.

America is being destroyed by these corrupt politicians and their Elite friends who head corporations and companies. They want a system that does not share the power and wealth with the people. Want proof? How many people know that many large companies do not even have to pay taxes? And many that do pay taxes get a tax cut and pay far less than their fair share. We are talking about companies and corporations which make millions and billions of dollars, and many do not even pay taxes, while others are getting tax cuts and pay far less than they should. Think this is an accident, a coincidence? Do you think that any politicians passing laws that have allowed this, are getting any money back from these companies that have saved a fortune in unpaid taxes? Get my point?

The tax standard for individual Americans is far higher and harder than it is for companies, why? These Elite have all the power, they make the laws, and are sharing the wealth with themselves while robbing the people, that is why. Again this is about their self-interests, it is not about doing their jobs. Corruption is about people misusing their jobs for their own self-interests and this is a very good example. Why are these companies not being taxed then? Where is the yearly missing trillion dollars then? What is the excuse? Is this responsible leadership? Clearly the laws have been written to benefit corrupt politicians and their friends in corporations. Just like with grey laws and the Patriot Act, they have passed laws which benefit themselves.

At the time that this 2.3 trillion dollars was declared missing, it was estimated to be 8,000 dollars for every man, woman, and child in America. This should give you some perspective. With that in mind is it any wonder that America has a national debt? And why do we have one? When this much money disappears it is obvious that corruption is the cause of our national debt, not America as a nation and most certainly not capitalism. America makes a very large amount of money yearly, so why are we not paying off the national debt, why in fact is it growing larger? When we make so much as a country we should not be going broke. Obviously corruption is the issue, anything else is an excuse and distraction. Corruption is the root problem of America and every other land.

This missing money would have been found by now if it were not for the fact that the people who are responsible for it, are the people who stole it, are the people who lost it, are the people who have given it to friends by over paying them for contracts. This is really where a very large amount of this money is going, If it had been ANYONE ELSE who had stolen this money, politicians would be finding out who did it, who is responsible. But as it is the money trail leads to themselves. Which would of course expose a vast web of corruption, and expose the connections between corrupt politicians and their friends with contracts working for government and a host of other money laundering schemes. In other words these politicians are not finding where the money has gone, because it has gone to themselves, and will lead to themselves. It is no wonder our country is going down hill, we are being made bankrupt by corruption and this is occurring every year. It is no wonder that criminals and crime are drawn to politics when this much money can be made simply by stealing. Especially when the people being stolen from are doing nothing about it. Give an inch take a mile.

And Americans are expecting corrupt politicians to put everything back into place? They expect politicians to take care of corruption issues within government obviously, or else the American people would be fixing it themselves. How realistic is this? If people are going to be this stupid and careless with their money then people are going to steal from them regardless of job-title. This is the world you live in, not the world you want to live in. And I bet these people who are letting this all happen lock their doors at night.

In other words you may not get Jeffrey Dahmer's viewpoint, or the Zodiac Killers psychology, but you lock the doors nonetheless based on their actions. Regardless of whether you understand these people or not, you believe, you see their actions and lock the doors and windows. Yet many can see the actions of these corrupt politicians, these Elite, yet do not believe because of a job-title. People are doing nothing about the obvious actions of these Elite, because of blind respect for their job-titles: there is a reason it is called "blind" respect. Of course these corrupt politicians think the masses are stupid, look at how easy it is for them to get away with everything. It is the conscious people who are being targeted by illegal programs written by corrupt politicians, not the blind of society.

Politicians don't see the ignorant as a threat because they pose none already. The ignorant of society are going on a label and stereotype of politician like this automatically tells you about the quality of the person you are dealing with. This is a stereotype, a simplified form of thinking, a short-cut to thinking, an avoidance issue of actually thinking, not a reality. It is a stupid way for determining truth. How stupid can anyone be? This is sloppy and laziness of the mind. Whatever it is it is no excuse for not seeing the Truth, and it is in fact an allowing of negative energy to build and grow, in this case corruption. This is just like any other situation in which revolution has happened, the masses are simply putting off the inevitable until there is no choice but to stand up for one's rights- just like revolutions of the past.

And of course the Elite know this and are prepared for this. That is what a No Fly List is for, Gang Stalking, classified technologies, COINTELPRO, Custodial Facilities, and many other things as well. In essence the American people have signed themselves up for the Path of Experience, for learning the hard way. The other end of it is that Americans are being very lazy minded, and since there are no observable effects, well then it must be that things are not as bad as they seem. Material, information like my book here is simply "hype". I have news for people like this, their way of thought here is about to catch up with them, and the effects are about to become very observable.

Because of the simplistic attitude of Americans these corrupt politicians and their friends feel that they are entitled to do what they want, feel that they are above all others, and so feel they are a class unto their own. They exist outside of everyone's box of thinking, because that is where people have put them by being non-thinking. As long as they exist outside of your "box of reality", they will always be too hard to see: you have already made up your mind about what reality is, therefore there can be nothing beyond this.

For many people what I write of here is crazy, which simply means they don't want to think about things, again it is lazy minded. It is because of this that the Elite get away with what they do. Quite obviously they feel that they are "the Elite" because they are allowed to do anything they want with impunity, so I refer to them this way throughout my book. In reality these people are crooks, criminals, organized crime throughout politics, government, and industry, and any other name is a distraction from the truth. When I speak of the Elite keep this definition in mind. This is not some far away kook talk, this is a simple matter of crime and criminals being drawn to easy money and easy power. This does NOT even begin to be difficult to understand. It is easy for these criminals because Americans and others across the world are too lazy, pathetic, and apathetic, to actually do anything about these criminals. The masses lack self-empowerment.

Thus criminals and psychopaths craving power and money are attracted to politics, and when that is your focus for taking a job it certainly does not even begin to be about serving people and representing people- this ought to be obvious. These people are about representing themselves, you need only look at the facts to see that this is true. And if you have doubts or do not believe, then assume it is true for a moment, and then look with these eyes- you will see that everything makes sense this way, because it is true.

We are talking about ORGANIZED CRIME within politics. We are talking about powerful psychopathic criminals- of course they are in government where all of the power is at, this type of person craves power and the abuse of it. And if you wonder at my statement of them being psychopathic, well what type of person lets entire countries be robbed and destroyed out of self-interest? Furthermore these corrupt people are united across international lines with others in other countries, like different Mob Families, and the proof is in the amount of international agreements in regards to many things.

I will list some examples and then move on. There is this quiet and avoidance of the fact that there will be an economic crash, there are international programs like Stalking, COINTELPRO, the No Fly List, and even Custodial Facilities built all around the world. There are even programs like Operation Clover Leaf, Chem Trails which is happening all over the world and this makes people sick and is obviously about experimenting on the world population. Furthermore it is run by the D.O.E. the last time I checked, is done all over the world, are we Americans paying for it? So if you need proof of a corrupt list of things being done, which shows an international link of corruption and agreement, you can start with those. People have got to start thinking like them and start understanding their mentality.

If we had responsible politicians we would not have the impending reality that we have now.

These corrupt politicians have no intentions of fixing anything that they have deliberately created, and in this case an economy crash. It would be self-defeating, why would they? They have simply taken the situation and now plan on making it work for themselves. To top it off these corrupt politicians are responsible for the building of these prison camps which are called Custodial Facilities and which I heard the government claim on radio as being, · "For a large flood of Mexican immigrants pouring across the border all at once". Anyone ever heard of such a thing? Think everyone will be running for America when the dollar crashes? Forget it. Yet this was on the radio, a cheap dumb excuse which insults everyone intelligence. Actually these are quite obviously in preparation for an angry American people. Obviously it will be the American peoples fault for being angry, not the corrupt politicians fault when the time comes. At least this is how these politicians are dealing with it. It is about misdirecting responsibility and guilt.

If they say something now about this economy collapse being a guaranteed thing based on basic economic realities, the American people will be furious and want to pursue justice now, and want to pursue these corrupt politicians NOW. If the economy collapses FIRST and then Americans find out, it will be too late to really do anything, as the government will suspend the constitution and declare martial law. It is an escape plan.

The real reason behind all of this will be for avoiding being caught and held responsible for destroying and bankrupting America, to avoid being caught for corruption never mind incompetence. Naturally martial law will never end until they know that they will not be held responsible for an economy crash, IT IS ALL ABOUT THEM KEEPING POWER. It is about having more power. In the chaos of an economy crash so many people will be in shock that they will not be thinking rationally enough to actually catch anyone. In fact people will be emotional not rational, and so corrupt politicians will get away in all of the chaos. These politicians will have a legitimate excuse for declaring martial law. Thus these corrupt politicians are waiting for it to happen so they can get away with everything. To top it off this American economy crash fits a larger agenda and larger goals which these Elite want. In my opinion once this economy collapse happens it will be too late for Americans and the rest of the world.

An economy crash is only the beginning.

Keep in mind that aside from corrupt politicians there is no reason why America should not be one of the richest nations on earth. If it were not for these corrupt politicians it would be. What makes these corrupt politicians so special? The people do, we do by turning a blind eye to all of this corruption. The people do all the work, these criminals get all of the money. The people's non-empowerment makes politics and government attractive, a Honey-Pot for crime and psychopaths. We can not take care of our national debt when we have corrupt politicians in charge of our money. Our government can not function properly with dysfunctional people within it, with corrupt government employees in charge of our country. Dysfunctional government employees means a dysfunctional government, take a good look at it because this is what it is these days: the quality of our government is the result of the quality of people within it.

At some point the American people are going to have to have a War Against Corruption and clean up their government and that time is quickly approaching. It is better that the American people begin doing it now before it is too late, and while they have a chance of stopping this economy crash and everything following it. By my estimation the American economy is designed to crash in 2012 or 2013- if it does not it will be a miracle. That said, if enough people become vocal and active, this can still be averted.

YOUR WORTHLESS DOLLAR: THE MAINSTREAM MEDIA IS A CORRUPT MEDIA- THE PROOF IS IN THE SILENCE: WHEN THE TIME COMES WE WILL BE SOLD THE "FAILINGS OF CAPITALISM AND AMERICA" TO DE-THRONE CAPITALISM AND DEMOCRACY, NOT THE TRUTH WHICH IS A CORRUPT GOVERNMENT AND CORRUPT MEDIA

This will happen when America can no longer pay the interest owed on the money owed, on the money borrowed. This will happen when the interest we owe, is more than our country makes in a year. Think about this. To top it off in early 2010 (I believe April) I heard on radio that this figure was at an 86% point. Meaning that there is only another 14% to go before the economy crashes. When we reach 100% this means that we can no longer pay the interest on the money we owe as a nation. This was not a big story on the radio only a few sentences and if you did not know about any of this, no doubt you had no idea of what was being spoken of in the first place. It was deliberately short and vague. Why? Because this is about the economic reality our country faces, these few sentences stated everything. THAT is why it was vague. THAT is the media's idea of important news coverage. Maybe I should get Paris Hilton to do an audio version of my book if you get the point.

Obviously the media is controlled for there to be such a lack of coverage over the guarantee of this. I just do not see that there can not be an economic crash, and I do not see that this can be avoided until it is addressed as the certainty it is. I would like to be wrong about this, but I do not think that I am. Like an alcoholic, until we deal with the reality of the situation we can not change it.

Larger elements of the media must be corrupt for such an obvious avoidance of important issues. The people in charge of it are obviously in league or a part of this Elite, and with so much money stolen yearly and the quiet about the inevitability of it this seems obvious enough. I do not see real reporting here and one has to look at motives if they are not. This does not mean that every reporter and his or her boss is in on this, but it does mean that people in key positions are. Why the unavoidable American economy collapse is not an issue, makes this obvious as it is the chiefs and owners that are calling the shots. They are not stating that this economic collapse is unavoidable, rather they are stating that they will "fix it", while simply waiting for it to occur. And as an extra point, if it does not start with America it will start with

Europe, and regardless will be worldwide and the result of corrupt politicians.

Too many people are relying on mainstream media to point out issues and are allowing the mainstream media to decide what is an issue, and what is not. Too many people are allowing the media to do their thinking for them. Are we thinking for ourselves at this point, or being TOLD what to think, and being told what is an issue or not? It needs to be the other way around, we need to be dictating to the media what we want to hear about. Again look at something as stupid as water-boarding, and whether it is torture or not. Another good example, is the idea that "Cows are contributors to Global-Warming". We are talking about methane and cow flatulence here Folks, how ridiculous is this as an issue? Cows are not the problem, PEOPLE obviously are. Until I see a cow driving a car, it will remain that way. Look at the amount of pollution we cause, need we point a finger anywhere else? Who came up with these dumb issues and ideas of "important topics"? The media did, that is who, and they are putting our focus on this junk. But I digress, back to the public turning a blind eye.

The American people are also to blame, the people are not being realistic about, or vigilant of, their representatives. They are not taking on their responsibility as Americans. They are not being self-empowered. They are also not caring enough to do something, to act out of concern. This has to do with the atmosphere of corruption and apathy that has been created, and this is also about the American people. Obviously the people do not care if they are going to ALLOW this to happen. The people are not taking responsibility for their country, their democracy or whatever system they live within across the world. They are not keeping it clean and functional, like the environment as an example.

If things are not kept clean and functional they deteriorate and stop functioning like any environment. This is lazy and irresponsible and will lead to even more robbery. And as you will experience, the people will be duped yet again when a new currency is adopted, unless people decide to do something about this impending economic crash. Deciding to do nothing, is still a choice, and will simply lead to things happening that you would NOT have chosen in the first place. That is rather the point, things have reached a tipping point, it is the quiet before the storm, and people have got to get busy. Currently we are on the Path of Experience.

Keep in mind that this America economy crash is going to affect the whole world. Where are the news stories and reporting on this? Who are we waiting for to take this up as an issue? The mainstream media, the government? The corrupt? Take a look, not one country and it's media is bringing up enough good points in regards to this entire mess, no one is looking at the root problem here, which is corruption and an impending economy crash because of it. The media is being controlled all across the world, quite obviously, why?

In one move these corrupt politicians will take all of the power and money from the people instead of being in trouble for bankrupting countries.

They will try to get the masses to buy into the idea that America does not work, and that capitalism does not work, which it does when politicians are not stealing all of the money. After an economic crash all of the hype about the failings of capitalism will be to take the blame away from corrupt politicians who orchestrated it all in the first place. They will say "Capitalism and democracy do not work", same as was done with communism when Soviet Russia broke apart. This will be advertised by the media non-stop like the non-American mantra it will be, and eventually will be about how we Americans and America need to "join the rest of the world" in a world economy and world government. People will then be robbed all over again as they are forced into a new currency in which they get only pennies on their dollars. It will be the greatest scam ever.

People will want to go along with it, out of FEAR AND SURVIVAL, because they will be poor- again part of a strategy. No doubt MICRO-CHIPS will be part of the solution, "Go along with this, or do not be part of our system", again SURVIVAL AND FEAR ISSUES used to intimidate people to go along and to buy into this dangerous plan. Of course the "benefit of eliminating theft and robbery" because of Micro-Chipping will be sold along with this: "You can not be robbed if money is all done with micro-chips", which is ironic because the whole thing will be orchestrated by thieves in the first place. Which will be the next part of the plan and robbery that these corrupt politicians try to put into place. These corrupt politicians in America and in other governments across the world want a One-World-System to consolidate all of the money, and to consolidate all of the control. They want this for themselves not for the people, but seeing as how they are hiding all of this information it should be obvious that their intentions are not good. It will be easier to steal from the people with socialism in place. They will skim the money, massive amounts, off of the top.

So shortly down the road Americans will be broke, as in have no money, and at that point many will no doubt finally be very pissed off with their elected officials. But by then it will be too late. Why didn't you care sooner? And who doesn't care about their country? You see it is a lot easier to say that you do care about your country, something that requires no effort, than it is to actually show that you care by doing something about it. If Americans are going to be this lazy about taking care of their country then this is going to happen, and has been happening all along. These corrupt politicians certainly get this, they get that most Americans talk this way, but few actually do care enough to want to look, or do anything about what is going on. How else do you think that these politicians are getting away with so much criminal activity? And to the point of running the most powerful country in the world into the ground? And I might point out bankrupting what is supposed to be and should be one of the richest countries in the world.

SOME POINTS AND EXAMPLES

Of course the Elite within corporations are involved as well in America's demise, and this is why we have had financial mishaps with car companies, and there will be more to come. The heads of these companies receive so much in bonuses and retirement-plans, that they are robbing the companies of their own money and profits. This is by design and is to cripple these companies, and to make capitalism look bad. It is a smaller version of what these corrupt politicians are doing to America- and this shows that these corporate leaders are in on the action with these corrupt politicians: it shows that corrupt corporate leaders are a part of this Elite. They are all working together to cause problems in America, to bankrupt it. Just like with America they are draining all of the money and resources from within until the companies implode, until the companies become bankrupt. The same formula used for bankrupting America. Coincidence?

When the amount of money these heads of companies receive lacks common sense, LACKS BUSINESS SENSE, lacks logic, and goes against the survival of the company itself, it is obvious. Think these corporate leaders do not know that they are bankrupting their own companies? How did they get the job in the first place then? Forget it. It is to put ownership of companies into the hands of the citizens who spend money trying to keep these companies afloat- which is all a farce. We are talking about paying debt by creating more debt- does this even make sense? And we are footing the bill for this deliberate thievery. They steal all of the money and then they say, "If you do not do something and support us, thousands of jobs will be lost and the economy will suffer", it sounds like blackmail because quite frankly that is what it is. It is all about robbery and bankrupting America. It is all about putting socialism into place- now the public is beginning to own companies, and this will no doubt continue to go on until the economy crashes. It is all about the people and public having to replace all of the stolen money. Furthermore by the public agreeing to this, we only encourage the behavior to happen again, it is simple psychology.

In both cases the financial resources are being deliberately drained to collapse the economy and car companies. It is the same formula, it is all a part of a bigger plan. And once socialism is in place it will be even easier to rob the people- at that point government will own all. You on the other hand will own next to nothing, with little future in sight, as capitalism will be non-existent and the idea of getting ahead in life will be a "lost dream". The "American Dream" will be finished. This is what happens when we turn our backs on corruption, and are too lazy-minded or afraid to even look honestly at what is going on in our government. This is what happens for turning our backs on reality. Reality being a government and media that is controlled by corrupt politicians, corrupt people, across the world.

The implementation of socialism will be so that these corrupt politicians own all of the money and power. Think that if "missing money" came out of politicians pay checks, that there would be any of these problems? Well if they like socialism so much, maybe that should be the solution.

Watch, there will be more things which happen favorable to public ownership, as this is part of a formula. A formula for socialism and the destruction of America from within. If you are familiar with history it sounds like communism, doesn't it? I wonder why? And to think that when the Berlin Wall came down they said that "Communism does not work"...

WHAT THE PEOPLE SHOULD DO: A SOLUTION AND SUMMARY OF THIS CHAPTER

At that time when the American economy crashes and the world economy with it, the American people and others across the world need to remain CALM and surprise these thieves by calling for new and instant elections and throwing these greedy crooks out. These corrupt politicians, this organized-crime in politics and industry, these Dementoids are expecting an emotional reaction, a non-thinking reaction, not a calm and logical approach to catching them. Thus if the masses remain calm this will throw a major monkey wrench into their plans. Having said that when the economy crashes these Elite may have a SECOND-EVENT PLANNED to distract the masses from a logical calm approach in the first place. When this second event happens the masses must still remain CALM AND FOCUSED and continue with their pursuit of these criminals. The masses must remain focused on getting to the bottom of what happened, regardless of world events and traumas, MK-Ultra on a global scale, regardless of events orchestrated for the very purpose of distracting the masses from their pursuit of justice.

It is that simple. Then the American people and other people across the world within their respective lands need to really investigate what has happened to all of the money and find out who has it and how. Everyone can start with the issue of why were we not informed of this coming situation until so late? Why are key points and issues STILL not being brought up? People newly elected under this crisis and because of it, who truly represent the American people and the people of their land, at this time of crisis will be able to get this done. They will be able to find answers and catch a lot of these people because when the time comes a lot of people involved in this corrupt nonsense will not be happy with the reality of it all. No doubt there will be people who sell-out once they are caught, there is no loyalty among thieves...And the important point is that newly elected officials will have TOTAL SUPPORT of their respective peoples. Think about it. This entire mess can be turned into a positive change as long as people take a conscious path. Remain calm and responsible, and these Elite and their plans will become screwed up.

When the time comes insist for new representatives, and insist on A War Against Corruption. Once this happens the people will no longer be divided and the root problem of our country, and the source of all of the other problems, will be addressed. AT THAT POINT REAL CHANGE WILL BEGIN. Cut off "the head of corruption" and the body will die. Corruption is the root problem in our world, anything else is a distraction. People have been deliberately divided, once the focus is put on the correct issue and people, it all falls down. Again the issue should be corruption and A War Against Corruption.,

Remember that positive action and positive energy counter negative action and negative energy. It is all about physics on a Human Level, what I call "Human Physics".

So with that in mind, be aware and informed, be self-empowered, be responsible, be active, speak out to others, and do your part to turn things around. When the time comes do not let yourselves be distracted and manipulated by world events, by world shocks and traumas. Stay focused on catching these criminals, and stay focused on love of your country. A conscious people, an aware people, a questioning people, a vigilant people, is a free people. It is the responsibility of citizens to clean up the corruption of government within their lands, not corrupt politicians. How much sense does it make otherwise? In the end people have got to discard their old ways of the Path of Experience and start following the Path of Consciousness: a conscious people is a free people.

CHAPTER 16
WHY SUCH A GOOD COUNTRY AND POWERFUL COUNTRY IS GOING DOWN-HILL: AMERICA THE "STANDARD-BEARER OF THE WORLD" IS BEING DELIBERATELY REVERSE-ENGINEERED INTO THE GROUND

Well like I've already said corruption is eating the country up from the inside, it's the final stage of any country or culture. If you don't believe it look at history. Having said that America is being deliberately destroyed from the inside, by corrupt, and by anyone's definition, selfish people. You can add psychotic, psychopathic, as well, as what other personality type could resort to such means for such gains, and at cost to the country and entire world?

Perhaps I'm getting ahead of myself here. I at least think most can and do agree corruption is a problem that creates more problems, however many no doubt will disagree as to how corrupt the system is. And many no doubt will disagree as to how deliberate corrupt politicians are being in destroying America. I don't doubt that there are those who find it hard to believe that America is being deliberately destroyed, reverse-engineered as a culture and country, as a beginning point for reverse-engineering the world: the level of corruption that exists is a result of people like this. BECAUSE people do not get the mentality and psychology of these people, and that is because they do not get psychopaths. However I think I can make some valid points to this though if you read on a bit further. I also was not a believer in such an idea as this, not at first. I had heard such ideas before but considered it cliche and kook-talk. What has anyone got to loose, aside from a few minutes of time? It is not as if I do not understand this viewpoint, I deal with someone like this EVERY DAY. In fact this exotic Dementoid, the Clown, is threatening and promising to kill me when agencies are not looking, think I am not properly motivated here?

But again why America? The reason why is that there are people in America who don't want to raise the standard of the world across the board, that would create greater equality and give all, the masses, greater power. Democracy is a distribution of power amongst the masses. America used to be a standard bearer for the world, now America has gone down hill. These corrupt politicians want more power and control, and want to consolidate power and control, rather than spread it out amongst the masses through democracy. Rather the idea is to destroy America, deliberately, and take the whole world down with it. Which in the end, as these corrupt politicians have planned, will lead to One World Government, the ultimate consolidation of power. It is of course a "power issue", something most of us can't understand without having rubbed shoulders with this type of person (I have), that's what all of this nonsense in the world is about. It is about discrediting democracy so that the people do want, believe, or have, a system in which they attain greater equality and power.

Remember democracy is a sharing of power amongst all, and a

dictatorship is a consolidating of power at the top: it is where a minority has all of the power. It is about people who are drawn to power and the misuse of power, people who get self-fulfillment from this sick behavior, which is how psychopaths are- the Clown is this way. All dictators are psychopaths, their obsessive pursuit of power stinks of this, and you need only look at what governments are doing now and preparing for, to see that the same kinds of people are in charge and calling the shots within government- and in other lands as well. This all points to their PROFILE, and points to the profile of psychopaths.

Like a rapist these kinds of people, dictators, have power issues and abuse of power issues, they get externalized fulfillment from this. As a result this has to be continuously fed like an addiction, because it is one. This points to the obvious profile of a psychopath. Psychopaths derive enjoyment from this type of behavior, and in order to have their enjoyment this requires "other people" for inflicting their cruel behavior on. They get enjoyment out of inflicting suffering, misery, and death: they get even more enjoyment by being out in the open and getting away with it. It is about their self-gratification. They are so far on the other side of the fence from where most people in this world are, that they are difficult to comprehend. THUS NO ONE CAN SEE THEM FOR WHAT THEY REALLY ARE. To quote the agents I deal with, "We exist right out in the open and people see us as they WANT TO SEE US, not as we really are", and this is how it is with these Elite, these psychopaths banded together within politics and corporations.

Again it is in my getting the Clown that I understand this type of person, the mentality and psychology of psychopaths and the Elite. At this point I can smell the stink of these people from a million miles away, I have been dealing with this type of person for so long. I get that people do not get this type of person, they are incredible and hard to believe, it took me YEARS to get this type of person.

Part of the problem for other people, the majority of the population, is the same problem I had: you can not try understanding these people based on who you are as a person, there is no comparison. If you are going to understand this type of person then you will have to start by looking at actions. You are also going to have to understand that these psychopaths do not like good people the way that good people do not like bad people, just like a Harry Potter book and this Voldemort character. Just as he hated "good people" and only spent time with those of a similar energy- evil people, so it is with these Elite. Psychopaths, just like anyone in this world, like people who have a similar energy. They spend time with other bad people as this is what is appealing to them based on human nature. Thus they will seek out and spend time with those of a similar nature and energy, it is only logical that people within government who are this way, would band together, unite together for their own selfish gains. Thus you have a logical cause for the existence of this Elite, especially when you get that it is all about greed. Even in their dealings amongst themselves I guarantee you everyone is watching everyone else. But back to democracy and the deliberate destroying of it.

So many corrupt politicians and governments of the world are concerned with more power not the people they represent- things in this world are deliberately reversed. Countries and cultures are being reverse engineered, taken down a downward-spiral. I understand this type of person due to my long years of suffering and analyzing sick and demented government Spooks, who have been wreaking havoc in my life for 18 years now, and specifically the last ten years. These people are again total power mongers, just on a smaller scale than what I call the Elite. The Elite are about more power for themselves, and if they are in government then this means centralizing it to take it away from the people. If you are going to do this on a world level then you need to get rid of the best example of democracy to prove that it does not work, because democracy is the sharing of power with others, it is the opposite of a dictatorship. Thus you have to reverse-engineer democracy, destroy it, so that people do not think it works, and you have to destroy the best example of it- America, to "prove this" on a world level.

This will be to end democracy and it will all sound like the falling apart of the USSR in the news when the time comes. It is all about these Elite destroying America because democracy is the sharing of power with the people, America sells this ideal, and they want the opposite. They will not just be destroying a country, but will be destroying a world symbol as well to totally convince people that democracy is a farce.

Just like the public I also didn't believe or get this type of person, or their psychology. Unfortunately I have had no choice but to do it, to look at and understand this type of person in order to try and put an end to my situation. I have spent years experiencing and analyzing the power-monger type, and sticking my mind into their sewer mentality to get a better understanding: and quite frankly it has been an uncomfortable mental journey. It is no wonder no one understands these types of people beyond a certain point: it is very uncomfortable to put ones mind there. Most peoples energy, their mindset and personality, is incapable of going there. I on the other hand have had no choice- so you can learn from my doing so, and take my word for it instead. I hope to put my experiences and knowledge to good use and hope to increase the awareness of this sick type of person, the power-monger, psychopaths with positions of power. Once people on a collective level start seeing these corrupt individuals and start understanding them, everything will change.

CHAPTER 17
THE MENTALITY OF THE ELITE: A DOWN-TO-EARTH LOOK AND EXPLANATION OF THESE PEOPLE: A LOOK AT THESE ELITE FROM A LAYMANS PERSPECTIVE

If we are ever going to understand the world we live in, it's problems, how they come about and why, we are going to have to understand the people in charge, their mentality. We should at least try, and if not we can simply look at actions- like my previous example in this book of the Zodiac Killer and others. This is a tricky one and has everything to do with why people living in this world can not see or understand what is really going on in front of their faces and why. Most of this has to do with the vast difference in mentality, mindset and brainwaves, between ordinary people- the majority of the world, and the people in charge- the Elite. These people are what I call power-mongers, and have a very different mentality than the average person. They are in fact psychopathic, psychopaths, and if you know psychology and look at actions this can be easily seen for what it is. Again when you look at dictators and how they act and are, and when you look at current preparations made by government, this all shows the same mentality, because we are speaking of the same type of person here. That said, one of the points of this book is to point out these people and to explain their mentality and psychology so that more people can see them clearly for what they are.

Now when we speak of the people in charge we are not referring to all politicians across the spectrum, of all politicians across the world, or even just politicians as corporate leaders are a part of this Elite. We are speaking of a great many of them though, corrupt politicians across the world, who like any organized crime or criminal organization, are working together for their own agendas, own power, own wealth. If we are going to understand this Elite, my word for the corrupt and powerful united together, we are going to have to start with the basics.

The first thing to understand, regardless of job title (stereotypes), is that these people are criminals. These people are criminals within the political system and as a result wield great power and influence. They wield power and influence over the masses. As a result they are able to buy out, influence, threaten, and own damn near anyone they want in any sector or walk of life. Their playground and breeding ground is the political food chain which is of course where all of the power, and as a result (If nothing else due to insider information and connections), all of the money is at. Money being another way to obtain more power and influence. As an example corporate leaders may not have the power of politicians, but they do have massive amounts of money if you get my point. And many of these corporate people are the Elite.

As an equivalent, think of Mob Families. These people want to move up within societies ranks, the social and power structure, for more power and influence, holding respectable job-titles all the while being corrupt and working for ulterior, behind the scene motives and agendas. All of which involve acquiring more wealth, and in the end more power. What is the difference? There is none, this just makes it easier to see these Elite.

Now seeing as how the playground and breeding ground is the political field, this makes it hard, very difficult for honest politicians to thrive. They are automatically entering a playing field that is slanted against them; the real players both hidden and seen are against them, and even the rules as a result are hidden. Honest politicians are entering a darkened room, where all is not as obvious as it seems. Again they are entering a room where the players are against them. Corrupt politicians with massive amounts of power and wealth do not want exposure, or their rules changed, the playing field cleaned up. This from their viewpoint is counter productive. This automatically would result in the eventual down fall of their power, influence, wealth, and the playing field itself. This would result in a playing field and game as it is meant to be played, with the actual rules in place, as opposed to a game which exists only for the sake of appearances. It would in fact result in a political system as it is meant to be, where the politicians actually represent the people, not their own self- interests.

In short it is that many honest politicians are on a team where their own team members are against them. Within the "team" there is actually "another team".

This is one of the problems. Good politicians do their job as it is meant to be, representing the people; corrupt politicians represent themselves. Corrupt politicians put themselves first and then the people, they are self-gratifying ego-maniacs whose world centers around power and wealth: wealth being just another means for obtaining more power. Any representing the people is SECONDARY for the corrupt, the Elite. First them, then the public. They have to maintain appearances for the public, in order to stay where they are. Having said that you can bet that much (if not all) of what they present to the masses, for the public, is secondary to their own goals and agendas, they are just making things work for themselves. Thus what they present to the public is secondary, an illusion, and therefore not what it seems to be. There is always going to be a secondary level, which is in fact the first level: that involving their own self interests. This is the real level, the first one, and is what remains hidden from the public eye. It has to remain hidden, the public would object to having criminals in charge.

Again a way of reaching an understanding, an equivalent of this, is to simply think of things in terms of known organized crime, the Mob. Imagine that they work themselves into the political system, that actual members of the Mob are now politicians, but in actuality Mob Bosses. How would they do things? What would the Mob do? Obviously they would maintain appearances for the public and masses, while secretly milking the system for more power and wealth. On the surface it would be one thing, while in reality it would be another. They would no doubt be misrepresenting the people for their own selfish ends. Any representing the people would no doubt be duo-fold, any laws being passed for the masses no doubt being part of a bigger scheme, a step towards an agenda of their own: more money and more power. Small steps toward their own agendas, being taken slowly and progressively, as a way of remaining invisible and not obvious. Small steps for their own agendas, involving the acquiring of more power, more wealth, while appearance-wise still looking good for the masses.

Now at some point in order to cheat the masses, within a free system-like a democracy or many a western nation, of their freedom and self-power, you are going to have to arrange circumstances so that you can bring the invisible power-monger level to the forefront. This happens when the power-mongers, the Elite, are ready to bring their level out into the open, and are ready to substitute their level for the level that is meant to be. A lot of arranged scenarios and false events happen and have happened, and will happen as a result of this. They are trying to push their paradigms into place, their level for the set-up of total control, which requires a dictatorship. THAT is what this economy collapse is for, and if we do not have one by some twist of fate, it will be something else instead.

Hitler used this and many others. It is standard operational procedure for the power-monger types, because it is what works on the masses. This is a matter of psychology on a collective-scale: MK-Ultra on a global scale. The masses are not contemplative enough to avoid falling into this trap which is why many refer to the masses as sheep. In order to avoid falling into this trap, the masses have got to be more reliant on their own thinking, and less reliant on others to do it for them. Especially when the masses are reliant on criminals to do it for them. Independent thinking is what counts, not externalized thinking, being thought for and told what to think, by someone else: which is what the media is doing and is misused for. As long as you are reliant on others for thought and truth you will always be manipulated which is what the media is misused for. My example of water-boarding being a good point- it should not even be an issue at all never mind in the media. In short this is the entire downfall of humanity. People have got to think for themselves and be independent with their own minds: self-empowered and self-thinking. This starts and begins on an individual level, it can start on no other. A collective of individual thinkers is a smarter, more conscious, and more free-people. Manipulation becomes a more difficult avenue of approach for power-mongers when this is the type of people they have to deal with. They are forced into honesty with a conscious people, and therefore will have less power. This is why so much in the media is a farce and lie, to dull our senses and to deliberately mislead us, to keep people less conscious. This is one of the reasons materialism is sold heavily through the television, as it is a distraction from our "inner selves", and therefore clear thinking.

So the Elite at some point have to bridge paradigms, have to bring their level into the forefront in order to take over and conquer the masses. THEY NEED AN EVENT, a cover-story and false pretense. It is all about power and to have total power they have to make a transition from being hidden to out in the open. The level of power they want can not be obtained otherwise. They do not want to spring the trap too early, to do so would result in large scale, across the board resistance. The shock of western style freedom to dictatorship would result in significant losses on their end, in the end P=B-C (As I learned in sociology the profits equals the benefits minus the costs). This must be done slowly and has been done slowly to negate the difference in systems and levels. This is to negate shock and backlash from the masses- it is all a manipulation. This entire transition of systems from the hidden to more obvious is currently going on. Until New World Order arrives and thus dictatorship, the Elite are still trying to be invisible to the masses, all the while their desired invisible system is breaking the surface and becoming extremely apparent for the free-thinkers, and self-empowered of society and the world. It most certainly is becoming obvious to patriots.

And as we get to this point of an economy collapse, the government is paying close attention to those who are outspoken about government, the people it considers the most likely to be fighting it, and for all of the right reasons. Again it gets down to targeting patriots and those against corruption. Look at the obvious signs.

But back to my earlier point of small steps for their own agendas, while still looking good appearance-wise for the masses.

The motivation for this is obvious, to hold their positions, their job-titles. Of course the ultimate goal would be to bring the entire system to a point where they no longer have to hide, can exist out in the open without ever having to worry about losing their power, thus able to do what they want. If you look throughout the course of history, this has happened many a time, these systems are called dictatorships- where the few rule the masses. There are many ways of getting to this type of system, but if you are dealing with countries where freedom, equality, the people, are the basics of the lands- like all westernized countries, then moving slowly and progressively is the best way to go.

From a power-monger point of view this would be the most intelligent path to follow, with the least amount of backlash from the public, the masses. Thus slowly reverse engineering freedom oriented governments into total control governments. Now seeing as how these corrupt politicians are united across the world in their criminal enterprises, like different Mob Families, they are working towards a uniting of these different branches, into one centralized family. Regardless of any infighting amongst various families and branches for power and control, these people have agreed to a basic goal, and have united for it. In this case, this is already being done and implemented, it is called New World Order.

New World Order is the uniting of these different political systems, with seemingly different politicians, under one banner, one flag. That said, in reality the hidden players are already united, it is just about bringing it out into the open. This is the centralizing of power and government on a global scale, which is what any dictatorship is about. Dictatorships, fascist-states are about the centralizing of power, taking it from the many, the masses, and putting it in the hands of the few. Thus New World Order is a plan for global dictatorship, the taking away of power from the masses on a global scale.

It is the opposite, the reversed form of democracy.

Western style nations are being deliberately reverse engineered for the sake of creating a dictatorship.

It is just that in this case these corrupt Elite want to turn the entire world into a dictatorship, not a single country. Once these New World Order countries are united, economic pressure alone will get all others to comply. Now keep in mind that behind the scenes these corrupt politicians across the world are working together for their own selfish egotistical desires, like any group of organized criminals. They are united by their criminality, they are organized crime. They are organized crime in the political field, thus the scale is different. This also has to do with the mentality of these corrupt politicians, the Elite, this world organized crime family.

This world organized crime family is far different from any Mob Family, or families, they are not as simple. They are like a particular religion, say Christianity as an example, with all of it's many different off-shoots, branches, variations. Or like a large corporation with separate arms or branches, with specific goals and functions. As an example of this point think of a car company that has separate branches, dealing with particular types, models, of cars. Just keep in mind that there are deeper and different levels with, and within, this demented group of nitwits.

Back to New World Order.

If you are going to have New World Order, uniting all of these different political systems under one banner, then you are going to have to level the playing field, creating one political system for all. Tricky right? No it is simple, and thanks to the government agents in my life I have come to understand this power-monger view point: their style, techniques, and "flavor". Uniting all these different political systems is going to be much easier than it seems. It is called economic collapse, and no doubt will begin in America, from there spreading across the world. So far we have had a taste of this (2008), as the Elite, this world organized crime family, fine tunes its plans for doing so. In order to level the playing field then America has to be brought down, and the American people have to be tricked into throwing out "being American", they have to be convinced that America does not work.

America is an example of freedom, democracy, and capitalism: as it is sold around the world. America is a good example of democracy and democracy is about distributing power and therefore equality. However this corrupt political playing field, with its corrupt politicians are about anything but "distributing equality". Distributing equality comes down to distributing power. With equality comes a higher standard of living, less polarity in this world, a spreading out and dispersing of power, as it is shared with all- again a higher standard of living comes down to a sharing of power. Democracy is a sharing of power, dispersing it amongst the masses: not a hoarding of power at the top of a political food chain. A dictatorship is the opposite of a democracy. People automatically wanting power, are against the masses, and in favor of a dictatorship, not democracy. By "proving" democracy does not work, this is like saying that "Sharing power with the Masses" does not work. So by bringing America down, from the inside, you can bring the world down and most certainly get people to accept a world government and socialism, it most certainly will be easier as there will be no example to the contrary.

America and what it stands for is counter productive for these Elite, these power-mongers.

If you are a corrupt politician, a power-monger, in order to have power you can not share it; by doing so you narrow the gap between the power you have and others. This is counter productive from a power-monger perspective, they want all of the power to themselves. Automatically you can find that the one system in which corrupt politicians, power-mongers, can thrive in and therefore the most desirable, is a dictatorship, a fascist-state. This is a system in which power is hoarded at the top of the political system, which is what power-mongers, by definition, are about. Thus at some point as power-mongers within a non-dictatorship system gain more and more in power and influence, the system they hide behind is going to have to collapse and be reformed to accommodate the hidden system. This is a natural evolution of the circumstances, it is actually de-evolution of the system being hidden behind. The real level, the one the corrupt do not want you to see (the one of their self-serving interests), begins to grow and over-shadow the very system it is hiding behind. This is what we are seeing now. In the end this is what the corrupt want anyhow. In the end power-mongers want, and exist best within, a dictatorship.

Can you imagine Hitler, Stalin, Idi Amin, Pol Pot, existing within a democracy, or any other western style type of government for very long? In secret to top it off? Of course not, these kinds of people, the corrupt and psychopathic, do not thrive under these conditions: they thrive under a dictatorship. At some point they would become obvious because their actions would speak for themselves, their actions would over-shadow their words. Kind of like what is happening now within many a western nation across the world. If we look at actions these days, we can see what is going on. Western style nations are indeed being reverse-engineered to fail.

The problem with doing this within western-nations is that not everyone is asleep. Thus as this hidden system begins to break the barrier, begins to emerge and surface, many people take note of it and begin to speak-out. Which is what healthy minded people who love their country do- like say patriots. Power-mongers do not want this, it is counter-productive to have people in society, cultures, lands, speaking out about the emergence of such a system, counter- productive to have "dissidents" within the land, so THEY BECOME TARGETED. Patriots are an obstacle to what these corrupt people want.

This has a lot to do with people and citizens being targeted by the Patriot Act- COINTELPRO, Stalking and Mobbing. My situation Mobbing, has a lot to do with things such as the No-Fly-List. Thus we do not have a lot of instant and potential "terrorists" but we do have a lot of people speaking out about government, and criticizing it, specifically things which are a result of corruption. THAT is why the No Fly List now has over a million people listed on it, and that is why the government lied about the figures and statistics when they were exposed for this. All of this is to centralize power, and to target individuals who are in the way- ie. patriots. This is about targeting people who are anti-corruption, anti-dictatorship, people who are pro-freedom and freedoms. People who love their land. This also makes these people into suspects, without them actually creating a crime. IT IS ABOUT A MENTALITY, AND TARGETING PEOPLE WITH A MENTALITY THAT IS IN THE WAY OF THIS ELITE. This all resembles Nazi Germany, except now "terrorist suspects" are the "Jews" (And as an important note: How the Jews were treated by other German citizens, is EXACTLY how people in Gang Stalking are treated). This all resembles the Red Scare except that now terrorist suspects are the communists. The Terrorism Scare IS the Red Scare all over again, and it is the SAME HAND-BOOK being used here. That people can not see this, is beyond me. In the meantime I continue to live the nightmare which other people in the near future will no doubt face.

But back to America, corrupt politicians and their plan of world control.

What to do? You take America as a world standard bearer, and bring it to it's knees. The purposes and intent are many fold, all of it "good logic" if you are a warped power-monger, a psychopath and Dementoid, in the first place. Remember these people only care about themselves, their life, their power and money, their health and well being, not the masses. The whole point is to make an example of America, to "prove" that democracy and capitalism do not work- THAT is why America is being targeted so heavily by these Elite. Capitalism due to the collapse of the dollar and America the country will be claimed to not work, to be dysfunctional in order to get people to accept socialism and to accept joining other countries in a world government. You can not have America exist as it is now and have this world government and world socialism, so America HAS TO GO. America is being deliberately sabotaged from within by its own corrupt politicians to not work: it is being reverse-engineered to collapse on itself and for the selfish reasons of corrupt politicians. The same is currently happening in Europe as well, and if Europe goes first it will all be the same as the plans are the same.

This way in the future only corrupt politicians can have the money and power, there will NEVER be a chance for normal people to become wealthy and independent. Therefore there will never be a threat to a corrupt system and therefore there will never be a threat to corrupt politicians ever again- as no one but politicians and government will have power and money. That is what this is all about, this is my explanation of the Elite and their plans in layman's terms, in a way that I hope that people can see and relate to.

CHAPTER 18
FLYING THE FRIENDLY SKIES- THE RESTRICTING AND SHUTTING DOWN OF THE AIRWAYS: THE NO-FLY-LIST- PEOPLE HAVE NOT CHANGED, THE GOVERNMENT HAS

In the future you can forget about flying anywhere. You can already see the signs, see this is happening, again it's being done slowly to desensitize and acclimate people to this warped reality. If it's done too quickly people will object in numbers, and publicly. That is why it is being done the way it is being done, because these sick people at the top of the food chain are smarter than that. Society at large and humanity, apparently are not. You are the frog in the pot being slowly cooked. You are Bugs Bunny in the large soup pot asking for some soap.

So how is it being done and what is it based on?

Well first of all there is a heavier police presence at many airports to acclimate you to martial law, a military-state, which will arrive in the near future based on an economic collapse. This is to acclimate people so police-state measures are more easily accepted when the time comes. Second of all there is a No-Fly-List allowing the American government to prevent people coming and going from America. It was said to contain a list of a few thousand names, people who for whatever reason were on this list. However in 2006 the television show "60 Minutes" got a hold of the list and it had somewhere around 44,000 names on it.

Does anyone honestly believe there are 44,000 terrorists, or potential terrorists running around America? All of a sudden since 9/11 these people have sprung up overnight? This is absurd, it is much more likely that the list is being kept for DIFFERENT REASONS, and that the "Criterion of being a Suspect" has nothing to do with being a terrorist suspect or a "security threat". The numbers point to this. So does the fact that UNTIL 9/11 THERE WERE ONLY 16 PEOPLE ON THIS LIST. This list has been developed and added to over time for use in the future, when flying will be heavily regulated.

I think really this list is merely growing day by day and is a list of people who are freedom oriented and outspoken against an obviously corrupt system, which by definition would be run by corrupt people: this list is about PATRIOTS. By definition these targeted people would also be in the way of corrupt people's plans. In all likelihood, this list is to control movement and to monitor these people the same way that Soviet Russia used to do- this is about "dissidents". Again this is looking more and more like a prequel to martial law which of course will lead to a dictatorship. Once the American government, run and controlled by corrupt politicians, institutes martial law, it will never take it back. Martial law will in and of itself be a prelude to dictatorship, and the end of democracy in America. No doubt an American people angry at government for an economic collapse, will suffice. As you may have noticed, the American government has yet to inform it's citizens of this coming economic collapse, yet has built prisons all across America, never mind that other governments are not speaking of this. This is called conspiracy, and it is conspiracy against the people.

The plan is for these criminals to eventually step out into the light of day (This is one idea at any rate, it depends on what choices they make- other plans involve them hiding behind a Spokes-Person), once they've achieved total power. In the meantime these criminals in government continue to hire criminals to do the work underneath them. This is the reason I have these corrupt government agents in my life, they are criminals working for criminals, in one sense. Each layer of crooked government employees has it's power and abuse of power issues and they are a perfect example of someone misusing and abusing job-title for their own personal ends. We are talking about power-mongers, people who want and crave power, and who can not have enough of it, and who ENJOY misusing and abusing it. THIS is what most people do not understand about this type of person. These people get ENJOYMENT and SELF-FULFILLMENT out of misusing their power and inflicting pain, suffering, misery. I know this from the Clown, as she is obviously a psychopath and obviously enjoys the same type of behavior for the same reasons. These Spooks in my life right now are very much like the Elite in one sense, the psychology of the person in charge is the same, and it has taken me a long time to get this type of person. So I get that this type of person is hard to understand, I went through this as well on a personal real life basis, but nonetheless I assure you that this is how it is. This is what I am trying to show and explain with this book. Hopefully by the time this book is finished some people will see and understand these type of people better. It is in knowing and seeing these people that we can neutralize them before they get us all locked up or killed.

Look at the agents I deal with in my life, and who are currently threatening to kill me to avoid being caught and exposed. These people are very different than the average person, keep in mind we are talking about criminals, criminals with badges and titles of authority. People put in charge for their personal defects, their psychotic tendencies. People without empathy. People who torture without reason other than their sick need for fulfillment; like any rapist this fulfillment is externalized and thus has to be re-fed over and over for the emotional high. They are morally and ethically disgusting, repugnant, and quite frankly evil. Their mentality and viewpoint of life is hard for the average person to understand. When I say "evil" I don't mean a cliche, I mean this literally. I have experienced things you can not imagine at the hands of these people, these Spooks.

As a result I have been forced to stick my head into their sewer-mentality as a way of self-defense for me and my family. I understand this type of person much more clearly, and way beyond the average person, but certainly can not relate to it. It took me many years to even believe that these people were real in regards to their mentality and what they were doing in my life. This type of mentality was too hard to grasp all at once, regardless of the nasty experiences I was going through. I may get to this later, it's extremely important to know and gives me a very good understanding of this type of mentality and psychology, of these Elite.

Getting back to the No-Fly-List.

Another point is all of the searching going on at airports. Again this is to desensitize and acclimate people, to get people used to having less rights, and in the end to accept this "New Normal": this warped reality that the Elite are creating for us.

It's corrupt NOT normal. It's to aclimate people to abuse of authority. When it happens to you, you may feel differently. This abuse, these "safety measures" are only going to get worse. Give an inch take a mile, and the people at the top want to take all. Still think all this policing and security is for your benefit? You might want to ask those who have been killed by "security" at the airport- which has happened and will happen again. How safe does that make you feel? How secure? "Who" is the threat to the American people at these airports? Maybe those security people need to be on the No-Fly- List because quite clearly they are a threat and disruption to the people at the airport. But you won't see that one happening. In fact I bet none of these security people received more than a reprimand, after all an atmosphere of blind-compliance to authority is what is being sought after by government, it's the real reason that none of these murderers with authority and badges ever gets in trouble. Murder is murder and if you go to the airport to catch a plane and then end up dead from "security" then someone needs to be charged with murder. But this is not happening. The government wants and is encouraging law enforcement to see the public as second-class and beneath them. Not people to be protected, but people to be controlled. This is also the attitude of this Elite and people in cults in regards to the masses. If security is killing people, citizens, and not being held accountable, then what is it really there for? Again this is about controlling people, scaring people into compliance, it is not about protecting people.

THE NEW MOTTO OF LAW-ENFORCEMENT IS: TO SERVE AND PROTECT GOVERNMENT.

Keep in mind that fascism is when government becomes cult. This is about blind-obedience and compliance to authority, no matter what.

Don't believe it? Have you noticed there is a rise in violent-abuse by authority figures? Have you noticed that the police across the country are becoming more brazen in where they are violating people and to what extent? In other words these corrupt police are now committing crimes against the public, crimes against humanity, in full view of the public: including murder because corruption is rampant. And unless they are videotaped they are getting away with it. At most it is usually a reprimand, a slap on the wrist: of course the police department involved always stands up for it's criminal employee, even in cases where murder has been committed. Pedophilia for that matter. Again for the sake of appearances and looks. Why not just do the right thing and put their employee in jail when he or she seriously breaks the laws? THIS would look best to the public. If an employee in any other walk of life commits a crime, what happens? They of course go to jail. If I work at McDonalds and kill a customer, I do not get to go free because I work at McDonalds. Only in law enforcement is fast-food-justice served to it's employees. Given my life circumstances I would know.

So how do you feel about all of this? What does your gut tell you in regards to all of this? Well let's take one more look at numbers, shall we, the No-Fly-List made for our "protection".

In 2008 the American Civil Liberties Union stated the list was now over one million people. Maybe you think 44,000 people is possible as a suspected security threat (how is beyond me) but ONE MILLION? Come on Folks! How blind can people be? How deaf? Wake up!

The people flying have not changed (nor have the people in our country), one million threats to air and national security did not suddenly pop-up overnight, the government changed.

This growing list of people on the No-Fly-List is a list of people who criminals in power feel threatened by, not the people. I don't feel threatened by the people at the airport (only by "Security" actually) and on the plane, or any where else in the country for that matter, but by the people in uniform in heavier and heavier presence, heavily armed, and capable of getting away with murder. In general if you can not be held accountable for murder I tend to be worried. So what's the deal? Don't be emotionally yanked around and manipulated by these criminals so that you are putting up with what they want, and set up for something later. Take a look at the argument I present and think about it. Believe what you want but 44,000 people is a total farce, one million people is totally ridiculous. What has changed, the people or the government, and where is the government headed? YOU DECIDE.

As one last added note here. Almost all of the people in Guantanamo Bay are suspects, and suspects only. Again I've discussed the reasons why and why they've never had a fair day in court; it's about propaganda and you don't see people in power giving a damn about the innocent. If you are a suspect and on the No-Fly-List, perhaps the next thing you should be worried about is prison camp. Think about it, one million suspects in prison camp, in Custodial Facilities which will feel like what they are once you are in one, prisons. These are unused prisons all across America which the government has acknowledged exist: and which are capable of holding millions (And they say there is not enough space in prisons, and that there are not enough prisons...). So think about this, after all you are a suspect if you are on the No-Fly-List. For that matter behind your back, just like there was with me, there may already be a giant smear campaign going on against you, and you do not even know it..Think about it and decide the kind of world you want to live in.

CHAPTER 19
THE INTERNET SHUTDOWN : THE NET HAS BROUGHT UNITY OF THE PEOPLE; IT'S GOT TO GO: AND THE WEEDING OUT OF ALTERNATIVE THINKING AND IDEAS: SO MUCH FOR THE FREE-FLOW OF IDEAS

Well this one is pretty easy to figure out once you understand how these people think. A divided people is a conquered people, the Internet has brought UNITY to the whole world. Therefore it has to go, has to be totally controlled so that unity is not a problem for those wanting to control the people. Apparently this is already planned.

Fortunately I came across some kids (in their twenties I'm guessing) on "You Tube" who came across someone on the inside of this nasty plan for shutting the Internet down. Although there will still be an Internet it won't even begin to resemble what we have today. It will be totally controlled and all alternative information and free thinking will be eliminated. A cable television system will be implemented, this is of course to shut down the free flow and free exchange of ideas. Go to "You Tube" while you still can and look up "2012: The Year The Internet Ends", you'll find the information you need there from a collective of young adults, from Belgium, and yes it is in English. I wondered how the Internet would be shut down, here I have found it is going to be heavily controlled to the point of being worthless. As an added note here the government Spooks I am dealing with have something on our computer so that certain information can not be found again or accessed, it's a filter of some sort, you can expect this in the future as well world-wide. People will have to come up with innovative ways of talking about subjects so they are not blocked and cut off. Or flat out banned from the Internet. Look at China on this one, except I live in Europe...

But back to the plan for controlling the Internet.

The idea is that there will be a basic fee for the Internet, enabling you to access certain sites etc. Like cable T.V. you will have a list of basics you can access for a general fee. However if you want to look at something else, somewhere else, you'll have to pay for this. Like an extra channel on cable T.V., say like HBO. I sure as hell don't have money for this kind of system. So a lot less people will be going to a lot less sites. As a result of less viewers, a lot of sites will lose their financial backing and eventually shut down. It's total control, so much will be wiped off the Internet.

The entire Internet will be reduced to pop culture.

This will totally break down the free flow of information and eliminate all sorts of information, almost from the beginning. The little guy will have no chance to exist on the Internet, and people like me will only be able to view junk for the mind, mainstream pop-crap. Which I won't, if I want junk for the mind I have television. Having said that I watch almost no television, I have a DVD player and usually watch something on DVD or nothing at all.

The idea is total control, and to destroy the unity and awareness that has come about world-wide between people of different lands, as a result of the Internet: because people are beginning to feel "united and connected" and without the supervision of corrupt government. People across the world are uniting on their own- a bad move for corrupt governments. The idea is to take away the one tool the masses have for interacting and uniting across the world. To destroy an excellent form of communications for the masses. This will happen in 2012 and no doubt be in conjunction with an economy collapse, in order to cut off communications amongst the masses. There is a reason why these Elite have chosen 2012, but let's stay with the Internet here. So what do you think? Plans have been made to change the Internet in 2012, the Internet is going to suck, and it will be changed for all the wrong reasons. Again you decide. In my opinion the Internet belongs to the people, the masses, and when the time comes people should be extremely vocal. On the other hand when the time comes, people will have much bigger worries as there are many other big plans for 2012 prepared by the Elite. Again we decide what will happen as well, simply by doing nothing, which is in and of itself a choice.

CHAPTER 20
RELIGION: A DIVIDED PEOPLE IS A CONQUERED PEOPLE

In regards to religion people need to put humanity first, HUMANITARIANISM first, and then the rest will naturally follow. A cleaner more caring, more honest world will come into being. All as a result of putting humanitarianism first. Humanitarianism is the root of all religions, was the original intent of religion, to unite humanity and bring it one level up, one step closer to the Source, to what many call God, Allah, the Divine. Even if you don't believe in the Divine, I think you can see the wisdom of putting humanitarianism first, indeed maybe even more so. Further more humanitarianism includes all, including atheists.

You will notice that now religions have become secular, dogmatic, corrupted. Religions have become clubs, teams, exclusive membership is required. This is opposite of the original intent of all religions: religions have been watered down and slowly reversed. Notice a pattern here, exclusiveness, team-ship, divide and conquer. Now (well for a long time- but religion is being deliberately manipulated again) people of different faiths are more polarized, more separated, and instead of reaching out to common ground as the faiths were meant to do, they are more divided and hostile, attacking and even killing one another at times. Again it is divide and conquer. A fanatic by any other name is still a fanatic, whether they hide themselves, cloak themselves in religion or not. The majority of people following their own particular faith would agree with this. Whether they be Christian or Muslim or any other faith; I am just picking the two being most polarized for manipulation in these times.

This division of religions is in fact to push people away from God, and into hatred. A divided people is a conquered people and in this case people who are supposed to be focused and rooted in God are being deliberately steered away from God, and very much of this being done by a corrupt-media that is being used and misused to incite and inflame religious division. God, the Divine, Allah is supposed to be the focus of religion, NOT HATRED, DIVISION, AND DIFFERENCES. This is being perpetrated and orchestrated by people who could care less about God, the Divine, Allah, but who see "goodness" and "good people" as being in the way. Thus they are trying to get good people who are rooted in God to fight amongst themselves rather than be against these corrupt people within governments orchestrating it all: the Elite of course.

Thus it is all divide and conquer, and the people falling for this ploy are not at all actually that rooted in God, or they would not be so easily swayed and suckered in the first place. They are being used. Again the root of all religions is humanitarianism.

Who amongst you would kill or attack another in front of the person of which your religion was founded on, sheerly because someone else does not follow your faith, your religion? Folks this is backwards, and absurd. As an example, would you kill in front of Jesus, Krishna, Buddha, or Mohammed?

These people were sent by the Source, God, the Divine, TO UNITE PEOPLE AS ONE and bring them back to God. To bring back humanitarianism to a race that has sunken and fallen, that has lost true vision for itself. They all came from the same Source, from the Divine, yet each religion acts as if it is "The One", which is a lie. This is short-sighted, ignorant, lazy, and totally on the surface. Totally backwards as well and totally by design. This is where people have hijacked religion and taken it away from God, Allah, the Divine, and taken it away from it's original intent. The real intent of religion is within us, not on the surface.

If Buddha, Mohammed, Jesus, and Krishna were in a room, do you really believe they would fight and attack one another to see who is the greatest, the "most correct"? Do you think they would fight over who is closest to God? This is absurd, anyone doing so IS FURTHEST REMOVED FROM GOD- you would expect this of kooky cults, not people of sound mind. It is ridiculous to even think it. God, the Source, the Divine, sent these great people of our race- the Human Race, through different time periods and places to unite mankind, NOT divide it. Certain members of mankind, power-mongers, the Elite, have used religion to divide mankind, and a lot of ignorant people have gone along with these reversed-intentions: this is reverse-engineering of religion. Say what you like but the intent of the Divine, the Source, is clear. This is why all religions are roads which end at the same destination. Anyone preaching or believing otherwise has taken a detour, fallen into a trap, and is serving someone else's goals- not the Divine's, God's, Allah's, the Source's. All religions are "Rivers leading to God".

These various prophets and enlightened beings have been sent across various regions, been born into certain areas throughout time, to unite people across the world under one flag and banner: that called God, the Divine, Allah. GOD by any other name is still GOD. Has everyone lost their minds? Obviously religion is being misused.

The Elite have existed for thousands of years keeping their backwards mentality and misused power alive: Suppressing, repressing, and infiltrating anything and anyone that poses a threat to them. Thus religion has been deliberately misused, abused, falsified, and mis-taught, from the inside out. This is how this Elite and power-mongers operate, they are corrupters and infiltrators of what is good and pure. Anything that is good and pure being an obstacle and in their way. Evil attacks goodness and if goodness does not fight back then evil triumphs: good can not survive if it does not fight for itself. There is a difference between being soft and being weak. Thus evil for a very long time now, and in present current time, is trying to divide and conquer goodness through religion. In many ways religion is being divided through east and west, "Christianity and Islam"- many people who claim to be followers of these faiths, are being divided, manipulated, and allowing themselves to be. These religions are being deliberately polarized.

Are you really practitioners of your faiths? If you are not practicing that which is good, humanitarianism, which is the root of all religions, then you are not. Religions should be practicing common ground not divide and conquer, which was and is the original intent of religion- to unify people and take them collectively closer to the Divine. Religion for some time now has lost its original meaning and purpose for the masses. In order for evil to flourish, good must perish, this is why. Thus religions have been corrupted and watered down to serve other people's interests and goals. People of faiths should not be oriented by an external form, by a type of religion, but rather oriented by goodness, actions, and compassion. They should be looking from person to person, not "faith to faith". In the end people should be united in goodness and anyone stepping outside of this, "Killing in the name of God, Jesus, Allah, whoever", should be recognized as NOT BEING RELIGIOUS, they should be recognized as merely claiming to be. In this way religions can not be divided and conquered against each other, and this also happens to be the Truth. Anyone killing in the name of God is not religious, they are merely FANATICS, claiming to be religious. Fanatics are a class unto their own, they are psychotic and stupid not representing any faith or religion. That anyone even turns such a thing into "religious issues" is beyond me.

Just to make things clear I don't think religion or people following religion are bad. I think the majority of religious people are good and try to do good, but these people are the keepers and shepherds of their own faith and religion. I think that those who are good need to start speaking out, and in keeping with the tenants of their religion, make sure their religion is properly represented. They also need to make sure, and work at keeping common ground with other religions. They all need to make sure that their faith and religion is not used and misused for divide and conquer of the masses, goodness, and religions.

Those who are good need to make sure their religion is not misrepresented for the sake of divide and conquer. Which is what the Elite of our world are trying to do today. Those who are religious and good need to make sure that tolerance, acceptance, peace, humanitarianism, and unity are the dominant characteristics of their faith, and make sure that those doing evil in the name of their religion, are put in proper context. No one committing atrocities out of religious ideology is a true believer and this issue needs to be addressed when such things happen...People who do so are against mankind, against God, Allah, the Source, the Divine. Fanatics who kill in the name of the Divine are merely wearing a label of religion, they are not actually religious. This applies to all religions and followers, whether they be Christians, Muslims, what have you: although as a separate issue "fighting for good" may be needed in the future. Religious people practice humanitarianism which is the root of all religions, people who kill in the name of the Divine, who kill in the name of a particular religion, are not religious, they are merely fanatics hiding under religion. And no matter what, a fanatic by any other name is still a fanatic.

Polarizing The People: East and West: The Misuse of Religion: Who is the Fanatic?

I wrote this after hearing a lot of ignorant people speak out against

Muslims around the anniversary date of 9/11. I could not believe the amount of ignorance that was being spoken, you would think that people would have more brains- or not. People like this are feeling what to think, not actually thinking first, and a lot are simply going with the flow because at least on this particular subject, being ignorant is fashionable and acceptable with many. It is stupid.

The patsies, Middle Easterners and supposed followers of Islam, were picked to foment BIGOTRY which makes people very easy to control, and a host of other reasons. There are very many reasons which I will not get into, and many details involved in such a sham (It's similar to "Wag the Dog", the movie) but suffice to say, anyone really of the religion of Islam, would not even begin to consider such an attack. Fanatics are fanatics, and these people were fanatics, NOT religious people- this ought to be clear. It is a deliberate ploy to divide the world, and especially Americans, in terms of west and east, and religion, like Christians and Muslims. It is a deliberate playing on stereotypes. IT IS TO POLARIZE PEOPLE, to create extremes amongst the masses for greater control, and for manipulations of the people down the road. You will note that America has much interest in the Middle East, and the population of America is much more supportive of the government in regards to the East after 9/11, these days.

Some points should be cleared up here. If you are truly a Muslim or Christian you do not do such a thing. Christians, fanatical ones (Actually they are Fanatics, not Christians), also commit murder, and other deviant things. Doctors who perform abortions are murdered by "Christians", people wearing religion as an excuse for committing atrocities. What's the logic here? Save the babies but kill them when they are older? Do you think Jesus would go running around with a gun shooting people he did not agree with? It is stupid. What about Mohammed? Needless to say such people are not actually Christian, merely wearing it as an excuse for their own warped mentality. I no more have a problem with Christians than I do with Muslims, which is to say I have a problem with neither. I judge people by their goodness, not a title or label.

These people are fanatics using religion as an excuse, and no matter how you slice it, a fanatic under any other name is still a fanatic. Religion is not the problem. So let's see things for what they are here and not be divided. A clear labeling, definition is required here: people committing terrorism are not religious, THEY ARE EXTREMISTS, FANATICS. People should not be divided over religious grounds, rather united over common ground and over a common enemy who is playing on religion, and therefore attacking religions.

RELIGIONS ARE NOT THE PROBLEM, FANATICS ARE, EXTREMISTS ARE. I am no more afraid of a Muslim than I am a Christian. Which is to say that I am not afraid of either, I see things for how they really are. Fanatics are the cause of these problems, NOT religions. This has to do with individuals, warped-sick people, not religions.

You have to look past the stereotype, the "job-title of religion", have to look deeper to see the Truth of the matter. Don't be lazy minded. Fanatics are responsible, not religion. People need to stop buying into stereotypes which are being sold through the media, a media run and controlled by the Elite. These Elite are playing on stereotypes through the media, and trying to get people to FEEL what to think, which is a diversion from actually thinking in the first place. These politicians and their other friends are power-mongers, interested in manipulating religions for their own ends. Many of the corrupt politicians are only too happy to play on this division of people and religions. Look at what was announced on the news on the tenth of September, and the timing of 9/11, that in and of itself should say something.

People have to look past the stereotype, the "job-title of religion", people have to look deeper, to see the Truth of the matter. Look at all of the missing money, look at how the Tobacco Industry started, now the Food-Chemical Industry, Chem-Trails and Project Clover Leaf, secret-technologies used against an unsuspecting public, the misuse of the media to promote dumb ideas and to program the public: these are thieves and murderers not politicians. They are their own fanatics, wearing job-title for their own selfish ends. Corruption is corruption regardless of what job you have and just because you are a decent person it does NOT mean that these people are. Just because you do not get their mentality it does not mean they do not exist. It is because of this kind of thinking that these people are able to get away with so much in the first place. You can look at their ACTIONS, and see that they should not be given the benefit of the doubt. People need to be self-thinking.

People allowing themselves to be manipulated over this issue of religion, are giving in to an emotional viewpoint that has nothing to do with reality. They are giving in to a stereotype being sold on the television and news, a stereotype being a shortcut for thinking, for lazy minded people. This is what a stereotype is, from an intelligent viewpoint and a truthful viewpoint. People out there are trying to manipulate how the masses think, through their emotions. Are you against Muslims as a result of 9/11? If you think this way YOU are giving in to bigotry, hate, and personal issues on your end- stereotypes sold to us through the media. That you can not see other bigger issues here is lazy-minded and means you do not want to look deeper and find out the Truth of the matter. What is stopping a lot of people here from looking deeper, is their EMOTIONS. For many this is simply a wanting to look down on others, a giving in to an emotional-viewpoint and then selecting information from this viewpoint without practicing observation, deduction, logic, and reasoning. Because people like the "feeling" they get by looking down on others and especially since this is not only accepted, but encouraged (like the Nazi citizens did in regards to Jewish citizens).

People like this are going with the flow because there are others out there with a similar viewpoint, and this "viewpoint", this schism and movement, is being encouraged by the media and people within corrupt-government. For people like this it feels good to look down on others with disdain, a "selected group". In short, people are not thinking rather people are feeling first, and to people like me THEY look like a fanatic. I could care less about their religion, THEY look like someone without a brain, without a clue, and are willing to be worked into such a viewpoint, and an emotional one at that. They are being worked up into attacking others, they are allowing themselves to be manipulated. They are emotional first, thinking second, and they "think" from this emotional viewpoint. They should be more honest with themselves, more questioning, and more logical. Fanatics are responsible and are the problem, not religions. The question is are you a fanatic willing to let yourself be whipped up into a frenzy for someone else's motives? I hope this clears things up for some people, we all need to be united. This is for those who I heard on the radio expressing their ignorance on the anniversary of 9/11. People like this do not begin to look deep enough and are actually a major part of the problem. It is because of non-questioning, non-thinking people, that we have so many problems in the first place. It is because of people like this that there are government programs like the one that I and my family are in. And to top it off our situation is even worse than most others. This is all the result of non-thinking and non-questioning people.

This is the world we live in not the one we want to live in. And until we as a people change things by choosing the Path of Consciousness, it will remain this way.

CHAPTER 21
THE WORLD ECONOMY PART TWO

Well early in 2010, listening to news on the radio, I heard an investor from the East being interviewed. He had clear insider information and this was not conveyed obviously but was conveyed deliberately, and in regards to the future world economy crash. He said that America and China would remain strong, that the dollar would not crash, because of America's connection with China. A deal is obviously worked out. America is one large entity/country, and therefore a deal worked out with one large country like America, makes sense, as opposed to many different countries of Europe in which there are many variables involved. The idea here is the safest most stable choice. It easier to work out a deal with one large country rather than many small ones.

He said that the Euro, the European currency, and Europe, would crash instead. And this makes sense, as they do not actually have enough gold, as I understand it, to back up their currency. This guy obviously had inside information, and I have watched knowingly.

Now Europe has had nothing but problems, since starting this Euro. The economies of various European countries have been on the verge of crashing repeatedly. No doubt most would never have had this problem if they had not gone in with the Euro. Yet it remains in place, stupid or deliberate?

Now I have also written a previous lengthy chapter about all of this as well: in regards to the dollar crashing. Is it all irrelevant then? No, there are many ideas and factors within this chapter which are still very valid, the information does not begin to be irrelevant. There will still be a world economy crash, and no doubt the dollar and America will plummet. Hard times are still ahead, and America may still be the one that causes this all.

As another point by speaking of the future we have the power to change it. The reverse of this, used by the corrupt, is that by "Hiding information about the Future" we can change it, thus as you can see there is indeed Truth to my statement. I believe that enough people speaking out have changed a few things in regards to this economy crash. Having said that this remains to be seen.

There are several things going on here, and I write about what is most probable to help make sure these things do not come to pass. But again there will be a world economy crash, it will be a mess, and there will be many problems and manipulations as a result. This world economy crash will still be the beginning of all, in terms of Elite plans. So my first chapter remains.

Having said that if you are paying attention the news is all about these days (Jan. 2011), the dollar, and China's economy and currency- this is all a sign. Obviously deals have been made behind the scenes, in which America and China will survive this world economy crash, by supporting each other. This is not hard to imagine with China expanding, and America being a land of many consumers. What will come to pass? I still believe that the my previous chapter on this subject can stand on it's own....

CHAPTER 22
THEORY OF CORRUPTAND POWERFUL PEOPLE- WHY DOESN'T THE AVERAGE PERSON BELIEVE?

"We exist right out in the open and people see us as they want to see us, not as we really are."- The Clown and her Buffoons, communicated to me in 2008

This is one of those subjects that is going to reoccur in this book. People always say "But why would they do that? I just can't believe it." and the thinking stops there. Like their question has answered all. Like it is all too difficult to really think about or understand, like I have brought up the intricacies, issues, and difficulties of how porcupines mate, as if it is rocket science and all that is hard to grasp. Allow me to make a few points.

First of all your understanding of people like this is not a prerequisite for seeing and hearing what is going on in this world. So if I say there are corrupt and powerful people trying to benefit themselves at the cost of humanity, that it is deliberate and planned, what exactly does your question answer: the "Why would they do that?" or "I don't believe it." thing? You are talking about not understanding the VIEWPOINT of these sick people and not being able to relate to the scenarios and circumstances that they create. That is normal but not looking and not hearing is NOT. Not even considering such possibilities is also irresponsible as a citizen and as a human-being. As long as we continue to respond this way these sick people will continue doing what they do. Why wouldn't they? When they see that they can make a lot of money, have a lot of power, and do what they want with impunity why wouldn't they? It is not as if these people are being caught; the masses make it easy for them by being lazy-minded and fearful of the Truth.

Corrupt powerful psychopaths do exist and unfortunately have positions of power because that is what attracted them in the first place; and unfortunately they exist within government, which is ironic when I look at other people's viewpoint. Psychopaths are attracted to power and the misuse of it, where else would you expect to find them? Government is a Honey Pot, a light in the dark attracting this very type of person because the masses are not vigilant and have made it easy for this type of person to thrive in government. People are blinded by a job-title and stereotype. The masses are not and have not been doing their jobs as citizens, making sure that their respective governments stay clean.

The people have set up an environment within their countries and governments conducive to this type of person existing within government. People do not want to trouble themselves, do not want to be responsible or are afraid and look the other way. And by doing this corrupt people see that they can get away with being corrupt, and within government at that. WE have to change things and WE have to start caring. Who else is going to clean up corruption within government, the corrupt politicians? It is corrupt because of them in the first place. How hard is it to understand that there are very corrupt and powerful people within government? How hard is it to figure out that they are going to band together, form a click and unite together for their own selfish self-interests and gains- when they can make more money this way? It is just like any criminal organization or drug click, it is about people of similar energy banding together and uniting their resources for their own self-gains. It is EASY to see and understand.

I assure you such people do exist, I'm dealing with some in my own life NOW and yes I understand how hard it is to grasp the mentality of people like this: never mind how unpleasant it is. That is because they are NOT NORMAL they are corrupt beyond most people's understanding, psychotic, the average person is not. It took me years to grasp and come to "relative terms" with people like this and their mindset. Normal they are not. Who they are is simply outside of most people's view of reality, however your not believing or understanding them, does not negate their existence. You can look at them in terms of who you are, you have to see them as THEY are, there is no way of relating to them from your point of view and how you are as a person. They exist outside of your view of reality and therefore remain unseen. They get away with doing what they do very often by being right out in the open which is too unbelievable.

However as an example we don't have to understand the mindset of the Zodiac Killer or Jeffrey Dahmer to see that there is something wrong with them. We have only to look at their actions and listen to their words to realize something is not right with these people. Again not understanding these people is not a prerequisite to seeing, hearing, and looking.

As an example there was a shooting in the city I live in, a very unusual event for around here. Several people died including a mother, it sucked. But the point is if you had been there you would not have stood there in denial, the great Idiot-Philosopher, wondering why they would or could do such a thing BEFORE reacting. You would have taken cover immediately, and contemplated psychology later…

It's ridiculous and counter-productive to living so the "Why would they do that?" argument is for someone less conscious. That argument doesn't fly with me. That line of thinking is for people who do not know how to survive, people like this are Darwin's Theory of Evolution waiting to happen. If you want to be intelligent you are going to have to start by looking at reality for what it is, and following it to its logical conclusions no matter if it makes you uncomfortable. Especially in regards to survival. Fear should not be an issue in your ability to look.

Now what happens when you take a psychopathic mindset, a lot of power and money, and network it with others of the same mindset? Think about this a moment. The level of craziness and insanity goes up several notches: this is what happened with Hitler, Pol Pot and others.

I imagine that manipulating entire segments of humanity and countries becomes the ultimate kicker and high for these people. Keep in mind that these people are into their own sick warped fulfillment regardless of cost to others, it is not about "others", it is about THEMSELVES and what they want. A lot of people like this actually get fulfillment, externalized fulfillment by harming others, they need to hurt others for getting their warped self-fulfillment: most can not understand this. Another thing that most citizens can not understand is that a lot of people like this do not like "good people" anymore than good people do not like "evil people"- this one I have learned based on personal experience and the Clown.

Caring about people, society, cultures, humanity, is not an agenda of these types. More power by way of manipulation, no matter the cost to innocent people, is the order of the day. It is part of their warped need for fulfillment. It is EXTERNALIZED-FULFILLMENT and since this is so and since we speak of powerful people who affect the world, this involves people like you and me. We are a part of their warped fulfillment whether we like it or not. We are OBJECTS to them.

To further their cause they corrupt others around them, the numbers grow and things slowly progress and avalanche as long term plans slowly come into fruition. As an example of this look at the economy in America and the world at this point. None of it happened by accident or coincidence and it's not finished yet. When the American economic system totally collapses it will be due to years and years of chipping away at it, although there is certainly a rush being made to get there these days. That's because these people are very near the end of fulfilling their plans of total control and power and they have a Deadline set for 2012 (early 2013) for reasons of their own. Not the least of which involves hiding their behavior behind a smokescreen of prophecies from around the world. They have plans in place for all of us and people have got to start putting out positive energy and positive action to change this. If we are going to live in a world we want to live in, we will have to start making positive actions and positive change.

CHAPTER 23
THE RICH AND POWERFUL: THE CORRUPT RICH AND POWERFUL : THE CORRUPT RICH AND POWERFUL UNITED TOGETHER- THE ELITE: THE ELITE AND "THEIR TEAM": AN EASIER WAY OF SEEING THESE PEOPLE

This one starts off easy enough but quickly turns into unbelievable for a lot of people. I understand, I used to be one of these people who scoffed at a lot of these ideas mentioned here. It was specifically my looking at the Tobacco Industry and Food-Chemical Industry that I realized there are people behind the scenes manipulating things with their power for their own ends and gains, and regardless of the costs to others. I realized that these people are out of touch with reality and for all intents and purposes, psychotic. What else would you call killing off large numbers of people by creating harmful deadly Industries such as the Tobacco Industry and Food Chemical Industry? Once I realized this I began looking and putting facts together. This book is my attempt to make a lot of these hard to get subjects easier to consider and understand.

This next chapter is a look at the group I call the Elite and their "Team", a very large group of people across the world who work for them, most of whom are corrupt people. The henchmen of the Elite who get the dirty work done. For all intents and purposes this Team is a fascist-cult which I also refer to as a world-cult, and the esoteric-nonsense that goes with it, I essentially ignore. The esoteric nonsense IS IRRELEVANT. A fanatic by any other name is still a fanatic. The cult-aspects of this Team is a sales-pitch, window-dressing for a particular type of person, the kind susceptible to cults and fascism in the first place. It is to attract a certain type of weak minded person: those who are easily corruptible. The kind of people who blindly throw themselves into a movement and cause. The Elite in fact plan on doing away with this Team when this Team has achieved all of the Elite's goals. My own end goal is to get more people to see the Truth of the matter here.

THE RICH AND POWERFUL

Like any movie, the rich and powerful need people to do the leg-work. This is simple enough to understand; the rich and powerful make decisions and pay others to carry out their plans to fulfillment. They can afford to, and their job, the "R and P" (the rich and powerful), involves making plans and schemes for more money, big money, for these people think big.

This is how rich and powerful people make money. The "small people" carry out the small steps, often unaware of the bigger picture; they are interested only in their paycheck, their money and job, and so get their job done. What work they are doing for their bosses is none of their business. In essence they are compartmentalized and only aware of their own role in the scheme of things. The "R and P" sit at the head of the spider-web and tie all of these smaller people with their individual goals and objectives, jobs, together: each one a singular piece of a puzzle. The "R and P" know what the puzzle looks like, know what the end result is supposed to be. If all goes well they will have an end result, picture, that is what they want. The end result being more money, and if you are into power more power as well.

Now keep in mind that having a lot of money translates to having power which is what I am really referring to here. There are other types of rich and powerful people who are into the "power-aspect" and reap money along the way as a result of their pursuit of power. In this case money is a side effect of the pursuit of power. There are clear differences and both legal and illegal versions of these types of people with money and power exist. For the sake of convenience I choose what is most efficient here, not covering all-possibilities, to do so would be wasteful.

Now don't forget that I am speaking of normal rich and powerful people, not the Elite who are corrupt and twisted beyond belief. People like this might head businesses, deal with the public in this context, but they would not do so at the cost of lives- most are this way. But as you can see, whether you are an honest "R and P" person, or a member of the Elite, small people are needed to get different things done in order to accomplish a goal, a business deal, which profits the "R and P". We will work our way up to the Elite and their Team, their henchmen who get the dirty work done.

So as I was saying these are only the rich and powerful we are talking about here, not the corrupt version. As people rise up the ladder options open up to them, they have room for playing life on another level. They have options available to them for experimenting and making money on a grander-scale. Thus a lot of "R and P" begin experimenting and branching out in terms of investments. Pop musicians, athletes, etc. are good examples of this: lines of clothing, perfume, shoes, sporting equipment, what have you. These people have power due to money, they are not necessarily after it and even if they are I speak of the legal ones here. A lot of rich people begin to step outside of their job-titles and begin to experiment with the idea of making more money on a grander scale. Making more money becomes the goal and in what ever way they think of, scheme, and co-create. The formula is consciousness, planning, and energy. These are not people who see the motto "I can do it" as an impossible dream. They believe in themselves and what they can do. They accomplish success because they know they can: these people are self-empowered which is what a lot of the masses are actually looking up to when they put these people on a pedestal. They are putting it outside of themselves instead of finding it within themselves.

This would be the problem of the masses who tend to worship those who "Can do It", putting it outside of themselves never realizing they can as well. The issue here is self-empowerment and action. Belief in oneself, planning, and energy invested in oneself and ones goals without harm to others.

But back to the rich and powerful and now the corrupt and rich and powerful.

THE CORRUPT RICH AND POWERFUL

Now we have another group to deal with, one more piece to add as we build our way up to an understanding of the Elite. We have been dealing with a legal version of the "R and P", now let's momentarily deal with the corrupt "R and P" people and then quickly from there get to the Elite.

If you are rich and powerful you may fall into the trap of temptation. Deciding that you can do as you will and deciding to break laws what have you; as a result of the money and power you have that comes with it. People like this may feel above the law and begin to do as they like, scheming illegally for profit. Or it can be as simple as being corrupt in the first place, getting involved in something that makes you rich and therefore powerful, and not getting caught. In other words perhaps from the beginning the individual was a greed-head hooked on the idea of money, lots of it, and decided to make money in whatever way one could.

If you are corrupt and "R and P", very good at what you do with a lot of potential, then an organized group of such individuals- corrupt and criminal, may approach you. These individuals being the Elite. They sit at the top of the food chain with an accumulation of knowledge and contacts, smaller people across the world. Thus they see individual corrupt "R and P" people rather quickly, like rising stars, and see their worth and value amongst the Elite. Another asset to the Demented Collective- a way for the Elite to gain more power as a group and more illegal contacts which translates to more power. Note that this approach is not about friendship but about business and power. There is nothing warm and friendly about this group they are cold-hearted businessmen, engaged in illegal operations like any organized crime family. These people ARE organized crime. So far most should not consider this a stretch of the imagination.

The Elite approach these individual corrupt "R and P" players and they become a part of the Elite organization or not. Those who refuse may be ganged up on, Mobbed on this higher level. The Elite wanting an individual's talents, skills, resources, contacts, and specialty of field working for them and a part of them. A rising star being a potential threat to their base of power, and cutting into their own action. They also see individuals amongst themselves, coalescing too much power as a threat as well. It is cut-throat but simple to understand. These are the type of people we are talking about here. Criminals and psychopaths with money and power. None of these Elite members want any one person obtaining more power, money, and control than they have.

As an example of a rising star who was approached by these people and who in fact did dealings with them, until he found out what they are really like, is George Green. He was an investment banker, a broker and dealer who was invited on-board with the Elite because of his specialty in field and ability to do very well at this. He sat in board rooms with politicians, business leaders, and corporate leaders for the sake of planning schemes to milk the masses. He eventually quit the Elite when he found out to what extent their corruption went. He found out how sick these people really are.

These are not merely people after money but people who have been corrupted all the way through- people twisted and perverse from power and their pursuit of it. As a result of quitting he was attacked collectively (Mobbed) by these Elite and "legally" at that, losing a lot of his fortune in the process as they whittled him down to size. Remember these Elite reside within the political-field and therefore have the legal system at their disposal. Which they used to their advantage to attack and destroy George Green which they did not do. He is now a very outspoken person in regards to these Elite.

Whereas there are people who are powerful as a result of having a lot of money, these Elite are after more and more power (not just money) and did not take George Green's quitting peacefully: Every new member counts as added strength, added contacts for schemes, added power. It is a good example of someone on the shady end of things who got invited to jump on board with the Elite because of his skills. However where we were talking about individual corrupt and powerful people we will now get to a collective of corrupt and powerful people, the Elite. This brings us to the Elite, and their version of reality. We are not talking about normal people here.

THE CORRUPT RICH AND POWERFUL UNITED TOGETHER: THE ELITE: ORGANIZED-CRIME AMONGST THE CORPORATE AND POLITICAL-FIELDS POWER-MONGERS: THE CONSTANT PURSUIT OF MORE POWER

The difference here in regards to the Elite is the playing field in which they exist and from where they manipulate from. People, the public, the masses around the world seem to think that corrupt politicians and corrupt heads of industry and companies are an isolated event, as opposed to being an organized group which is ridiculous to consider. It might make us more comfortable to think this, but the odds are against a group of organized criminals not being formed within the political-system where so much money, power, and temptation, exists in the first place. Quite frankly this is what attracts a lot of these warped individuals to begin with. Just like a drug click they seek out others of a similar vibe and of similar habits.

A lot of these warped individuals in their climb for power and money choose the political-field because this is where the ultimate form of power is at and is what no doubt corrupts other politicians who went in clean, but perhaps were not strong enough in character. It is logical to assume (indeed against the odds for it to be different) that as these corrupt individuals rub shoulders in government that they are going to work together to obtain more money and more power. There is strength in numbers and thus of course a group of like-minded corrupt politicians will band together. Think of a group of thieves banding together to start a car-theft-ring for more money or a bunch of drug-users forming their own click so there is always something to smoke.

Naturally corrupt individuals within government are going to band together and pool resources, it is ridiculous to think otherwise and this means a group is formed, a COLLECTIVE. It is in fact organized crime within the political sector and political playing-field. We are talking about criminals who pose as politicians. We are talking about a gang of them within politics, within government, like a gang of bullies at the school. We are talking about people who use their job-title, jobs within government to their own advantages and who use their high positions of authority to establish contacts and connections within other fields and sectors of life. They do this to make more money and to have more power by banding together, by uniting together, by networking. They also network with others outside of the political playing-field.

This is what lobbying does as an example. It allows these political criminals to intermingle with other crooks, other players from other walks of life. Like say businessmen: heads of industry, heads of corporations, heads of business's etc., where a lot of the money and power is at. Lobbying is institutionalized bribery for this very reason. Schemes, plans, deals, money, are made and exchanged for promises. This would all be ILLEGAL except these politicians make deals to pass laws so that what is wanted by big business leaders becomes not illegal. Like say large corporations not having to pay taxes if you see what I mean. Later down the road the politicians "helping out" get rewards, perks, money and power, and influence as a way of reciprocation. Like with the Food-Chemical Industry in which politicians are members of these companies, affiliated with them in some way. Through these companies the politicians receive money- they get over-paid at these companies as a way of being PAID OFF. It is a system of pay-offs for favors and money.

As an example these Elite in politics make deals with heads of industry and companies who are also corrupt and who are hired by government and deliberately over-paid by government for their services. Later the corrupt politicians get some of this extra over-paid money from their friends heading these over-paid companies with over-paid government contracts, thus we have trillions of dollars missing yearly. It is theft from the American people and money laundering. It is all about money-laundering, bribery, and all illegal. Or at least it WOULD BE if people would really catch on to this. The people are not holding this Elite accountable. It is all a buffet table for corrupt-individuals within government. It is also a way for them to meet and incorporate people from outside of politics into their club, group, gang, organization- thus the Elite unfortunately are also heads of corporations, industries, and businesses. The corruption spreads like a disease, it is the weakness and desire of these individuals, their quest for power.

We are not talking about people who are simply rich and powerful or simply corrupt rich and powerful individuals, we are talking about an organization of this type of person. I hope this makes a point for the existence of a group of corrupt powerful individuals, banded and united together for more power and money. I hope this clearly illustrates the corruption within government and how it works- none of this is far-fetched. It is actually common sense, evolution in one sense given the circumstances which do exist.

The government and blindness of the masses makes it all a honey-pot for criminals and psychopaths. To think that there are a few random criminals within government, a few corrupt business leaders here and there, individuals doing it on their own, is not very realistic. If you look at the political system where many of these Elite are, the actual political system is set up to favor them and their corruption and corrupt practices. Again lobbying is a perfect example of this. Only corrupt individuals banded together would set up such a scheme within government and take advantage of such a system in the first place. How hard is this to see? You think it is coincidence? Why, because it makes you uncomfortable? Your being afraid to look at the Truth is not going to change it or reality. Only awareness, consciousness and action, will change things for the better. Self-empowerment is key for changing all of this. Only the people can, and only by being self-empowered.

Now to get back to my earlier comparison of different types of people with money and power. The rich and powerful, the corrupt-rich and powerful, and now the Elite. These Elite are after power which separates them from other types of people who have money and power as a result of money. They are also separated from many in terms of being united together as an organization. No doubt there are many rich and powerful who are net-worked together to make a healthy profit, legal-business-deals, but this is not the type of people we are talking about here. We are talking about the Elite whos' mentality is very different from most others. They are cold, ruthless, corrupt, and constantly on a pursuit of more power: life and people are like a big Monopoly game for them.

These Elite operate differently from the "R and P" and former athletes, pop-musicians, what-have-you, branching out to make more money in a different way and scale. They have entirely different options open to them due to their position in life; the political and corporate playing-field. They are corrupt beyond belief, their minds twisted and bent with their pursuit of power and level and degree of power, thus they are all together another breed and level to understand. The creation of the Tobacco Industry and Food-Chemical Industry are good examples of this. These are also good examples of their pursuit of power and money at all costs, at the cost of the lives of others. To top it off their playing-field affects entire populations which is a heady mix.

Now as with the "R and P" the Elite need people to do the dirty work, henchmen, a Team. Seeing as how the Elite is a group of one particular mental type, cold, heartless, ruthless, corrupt, and illegal, they need a team of a similar mindset. Hiring priests, nuns, good Samaritans, will not work: hiring criminals, degenerates, people from all walks of illegal life will. Thus corrupt people are going to do the leg-work of the Elite. By logic, evolution of thought, we can see that this Team is corrupt. It is logical that the Elite have this Team and that this Team is this way. Criminals hire other criminals to do their work.

The Elite like any "R and P" also do not inform these smaller people of the larger scheme of plans, they only tell these people of their own particular part, what they need to know to get their job done. They are compartmentalized to keep secrecy and the larger scheme of things is none of their business. Now having said that, this Team and the Elite, are a bit different on a few points, very different than most other people. To some extent this Elite Team does know of the Elite's plans for humanity, it is just that this Team does not know that it will be eliminated by the Elite, for very clear cut-throat reasons.

For starters the Elite have molded this Team into an organization, a movement of it's own. Using the psychology involved in creating fascism and cults which has been perfected by government, they have created a group of hard-core fanatics willing to do extreme things. This is the psychology used in creating a collective with a single mind and vision- which is what fascist movements and cults are. They are given a "purpose". In Star Trek terms we are talking about creating the Borg. Members, individuals of fascist-movements and cults, being called fanatics. There are several layers to this Team as well.

Suffice to say this Team is a group of fanatics who are some what privy to the Elite's plans, and believe it or not are sold on a world goal to give this Team a sense of common purpose, cohesiveness, and a collective objective- to give them unity and a core-belief system. This is about giving this Team a collective form of self-identity as well. These people, this Team, has been sold a bunch of lies by the Elite just like anyone else these Elite deal with to get the job done. In short this Team can be thought of as a fascist movement which is the same as cult. A fascist movement with a world-goal, one-world under their rule which is typical of any fascist movement in the first place. And this one world under their rule, unknown to this Team, is what the Elite want for themselves. Like any fascist movement, just like with my Mobbing, these people are only being used for what the leaders want without actually knowing what the real intent and real plans are.

Now as I mentioned before, due to the playing-field this Elite has options open to them for playing Monopoly that most others do not. This also means that they have a wide range of small people, henchmen, working for them across the spectrum. Having said that not all people who work for the Elite are willing participants, not all even knowledgeable that they are being used.

Since corrupt politicians are involved this means they have the legal system at their disposal and all that goes with it as an example. This means that government employees of all backgrounds, good-politicians, agents of various agencies, and police alike fall under the Elite's sway. Compartmentalization is a part of the job for these people, part of their discipline for those in the legal system, and they with their resources (spying, technology, informants), either willingly or unwittingly work for the Elite as needed. When it is already part of the job a lot of questions will not be asked. In other words some are corrupt working for this Team within their job-titles, but the rest are not, they are merely following orders happy with their job and what they do- they do not know any better. This is one of the advantages the Elite have over others and is a good example of their resources which they pool together.

The Elite know what their plans are in any given scheme, these small people, government and legal-people do not. The difference between a sheep and a dog is power, and a little bit of knowledge, NOT blindness. Now to other points.

The end result for these Elite, in regards to plans, is always more power and control (like the Mob Family comparison), control going hand in hand with power. A world economic crash followed by New World Order being pushed for by the Elite and their Team is a good example of this. It is the ultimate Con-Job and ultimate grab for power. Again due to options available at their level, and their corruption, they think, live, and act differently from those who are simply rich and powerful- or anyone else for that matter. They are corrupt, act as a collective and are totally hooked and addicted to power. They are also psychotic, so distanced from reality that they are willing to cook up schemes which are responsible for hurting and killing people, LARGE NUMBERS OF PEOPLE for the sake of their own gain. From all of the possibilities they choose things repeatedly, schemes, which are to the detriment of the masses. They are attacking the masses. Their ACTIONS show this, they are insane from any observant intelligent viewpoint. Naturally they are going to hide this. That said it is hidden in plain sight and right out in the open. How people can not see it in the first place is beyond me.

Having said that they are sloppy due to arrogance, occasionally being obvious, and these days they are being noticed more as they try to push their plans with a 2012/13 deadline into place. The other thing is that the type of new political system they have chosen is starting to break the surface as they approach the time for when they will put it in place- 2012 (early 2013) is when it will all start. It is becoming visible, this new political and economic system as they make some basic preparations for putting it into place, as they begin to slowly integrate it with the current failing sabotaged system for reasons and benefits of their own. I speak specifically of socialism which is constantly pushed in America these days. It will also be pushed for the world as a cure to the failed world economy which will collapse as a result of America crashing, or possibly Europe. It will be easier to skim money off the top with socialism in place. They will have all money and all power at their disposal with this system in place. This is the only reason why these governments around the world have not announced to their own people that this will happen. They will deliberately crash the world economic system and then offer a cure, a solution which benefits themselves.

All of these corrupt political figures around the world are deliberately keeping their mouths shut for their own gain and committing conspiracy against their own people. This is an obvious economic crisis, it will happen, it has to based on simple economics: all of these governments know, just not the people. Their keeping quiet means they want it to happen, and have all agreed to let it happen. In my opinion it is for creating One World Government, a One World Economic System, a New World Order. During this state of shock across the world, once the world has been traumatized by economic-crashes, there will be rioting and fighting. It is inconceivable to believe that these corrupt leaders across the world are not prepared for this, thus something will happen yet again, something big, captivating, traumatizing, to steer people where these Elite want them. These world traumas will be for greater control of the masses- it will be to steer the masses into a particular direction, one which these Elite want. The same way that ranchers might use guns and dogs to steer their herd of cattle into a corral. It is to get people emotional and non-thinking.

The masses have no idea, for some reason this is too difficult to see, yet it is easy enough to see and understand when you try and follow LOGIC to it's natural conclusion. Again logic, observation, reasoning, and deduction (L.O.R.D.) are key for seeing the world around you as it really is. Again if something is brought up about something that is hidden you do not have to reinvent the wheel, simply be your own detective as this works. If you look you will see this Elite and their plans, I hope this helps.

CHAPTER 24
CORRUPTION: A SUMMARY OF WHAT TO DO: CITIZENS, THE PEOPLE, AGENTS AND POLITICIANS: UNITING IN GOODNESS AND FIGHTING BACK: A MATTER OF ENERGY AND BALANCE: "HUMAN PHYSICS"

When the economy collapses there will be a lot of angry people, a good many of them angry because they were not informed and ignorant. This has to do with people choosing to be blind about the world they live in as there are a lot of signs of what is to come. As is typical many people want to believe that they live in a world that does not actually exist. They believe in what they are sold in the media (which is controlled) and by politicians. They feel more comfortable believing in this imaginary world as the reality is more scary. They choose to believe in a world that they want to exist yet does not. Until people begin looking and seeing, begin seeing clearly and start dealing with obvious problems like corruption, this will always be a world which is less then they believe. If you are going to change things for the better you first have to identify the problem- just like with an alcohol problem for example. If you want a better world then you have to work for it and put in time and positive energy for positive change. Until then this is the world you live in, not the world you want to live in. There will have to be A War Against Corruption if things are ever going to get better and improve in this world.

Pursuing justice meaning that people will have to re-elect officials, call for instant and new elections, and go after those in government who allowed such an economic crash to occur in the first place. As at the least they were incompetent at performing their jobs and in reality corrupt. And the theme will have to be corruption as America is supposed to be one of the richest most powerful countries in the world yet somehow will be broke. It isn't being spent on the people, I guarantee you it is going to this Elite. Think they will be uncomfortable and have something to worry about? Not hardly, unlike most of the world they will already be prepared. The proof of this is in the silence- thus a War Against Corruption is needed and will be needed when the time comes.

These Elite want a big world trauma, it is what they have set up all of this infra-structure for of Custodial Facilities (prisons), Stalking (a Citizen Police Force), the Patriot Act (COINTELPRO), the No Fly List (like the USSR), and many other things as well. It is ALL the groundwork and set up for total control for when an excuse is created- a large world trauma, MK-Ultra on a global scale. Clearly this Elite want this, they have spent enough time preparing for it and the economy has been quite deliberately robbed and neglected to the point of it looking like their chosen event.

Again this is a possibility as this also depends on the people. With that in mind I provide the following piece I wrote three or four years ago. This brings up the issue of energy and balance and doing what is right. This brings up the issue of action and non-action within a certain context, as we all may have no choice in this. It is the nature of these people to make choices for us based on their own self-interests. This is what I am experiencing in my own life with people of a similar mentality, even without that it is still easy to figure out and see.

ACTION AND NON-ACTION: GOOD AND EVIL: BEING GOOD DOES NOT MEAN BEING WEAK: THE LAW OF CAUSE AND EFFECT ON A HUMAN LEVEL- "HUMAN PHYSICS", AN EASIER WAY TO SEE AND UNDERSTAND THINGS

You are a good person and New World Order comes rolling around. They tell you you have to go with them. Maybe they give you an excuse maybe they just take you to a camp. Or maybe it is your neighbors who are taken.

What will you do, what will your neighbors do? Be enslaved at a camp, a Custodial Facility where they may put you to work or kill you? What is the purpose of these camps? How similar will these be to Guantanamo Bay? Obviously the purpose is to lock up those who are resistant to the governments overthrow of the people when the economy crashes (or some other event) and martial law is declared. All of this looking the other way at that point will not work as there will finally be action being taken by these Elite- and against the people and out in the open for all to see. At that point there will be no looking the other way. Passivity at that point will not work. America will have reached a point where the government has decided it is "We the government" not "We the people" and at that point Americans will have to fight for freedom and democracy all over again. And I might point out this would not even be possible if the Constitution had been adhered to. This is what the Terrorism Scare, the Red Scare of our times was created for: for over-throwing the Constitution. Again the politicians are fallible, the Constitution is not.

Now everyone has a right to question things. If you are good and against corruption, fascism, abuse of power, or simply believe in America as it was founded and meant to be, then you will have to fight, there will not be much choice once they start rounding people up. Hoping for the better at that point will be stupid if the government has decided to take action. Think about that word FREEDOM and what it really means to you, especially since it is the heart and soul of our country. Think about how much you take it for granted: I couldn't take it for granted if I tried, I have lived without it for 18 years thanks to illegal government programs. Based on what is going on in my life I see what government is doing and is up to, I know what people are in for down the road here. No doubt many are in for a life like mine and my family's, it will be like the rise of Hitler all over again. Look at the groundwork being laid down, it already is.

If things get as far as I have just described then violence, that no-no word, will be necessary at that point. Things are already near that point because too many people have been blind, lazy, ignorant, and fearful: people have been walking on the Path of Experience. And the longer people sit back on their butts now the more extreme it will have to be later.

This is a matter of energy, physics on a human level, but it is still about the law of cause and effect. It will take an equal amount of positive reaction and energy to change all of this growing negative energy and actions by corrupt government employees. When negative energy builds, a counter active energy takes place to balance it. This is a law of the universe, the law of cause and effect, it is Divine Law. For every action there is an equal opposite reaction. In the beginning lesser energies are required to balance things out. If positive energies do nothing, in this case people and positive actions, then the negative energy slowly builds like snow on a mountain side, an avalanche waiting to happen. Give an inch take a mile. In the end if there is too much inactivity and cowardice then a final point will be reached. All of the small accumulative non-action will result in one big mass of action- an avalanche, revolution. It will take a very large amount of energy at that point to counter act everything that has been going on, to counter act all of the negative energy and action. And at that point in time people will not be given a choice.

History speaks for itself.

In terms of past history people have ended up fighting their governments because they ignored the corruption within them until they had to take action. The people tried living in denial, being lazy minded, non-conscious, non-active, and apathetic. Sound familiar? I can not think of an example where this is not the case, including present times.

The masses ignored the corruption and abuse of government until they were forced into taking action which is called revolution. In all cases the masses wanted to ignore things, the Path of Experience, until they had no choice but to deal with the problem. They did not want the responsibility for their own lives. They wanted to look the other way and not deal with things consciously or intelligently, they wanted someone else to do this for them. Sound familiar? Thus the negative energy and negative actions of corruption slowly built up until people were forced to take action- and usually at a point when the corruption began to totally infringe on their freedom and existence.

In this case in order to compensate for all of the negative energy which built up slowly over time, a large amount of positive energy and action, all things being relative here, was needed to re-balance the problem. An instant avalanche of action occurred. Thus throughout history there have been revolutions and people fighting their governments , the law of cause and effect, balance of energy- Human Physics, and it looks like we are going to make the same mistakes of our ancestors. That said we are different than our ancestors and we have the power to change things as humanity is beginning to wake up. We must counter and balance the negative people and negative energy with positive action and energy or else it will all continue to grow. It all gets down to the Path of Experience and the Path of Consciousness. Change can be made in a peaceful manner without violent fighting and without revolution.

This means taking personal responsibility and not waiting for others to fix things, like say corrupt politicians. If you start from the beginning then it requires less energy as I have illustrated with my chapter on the Path of Experience and Consciousness. It is all about energy and physics on a human level. Why not start trying to fix things now?

In the end the root problem with the masses is that they are not self-empowered and not self-thinking. THIS is and has been the problem for thousands of years and this is what has led to the build-up of negative energy throughout the ages. What is so different about our times that people can not see the reality we face? Absolutely nothing and that is the point, many non-thinking and non-empowered people are causing this to happen all over again. More people need to wake up.

A New Revolution is needed here, a re-balancing of energy but in a peaceful way and on a peaceful scale. The Path of Experience needs to be discarded and the Path of Consciousness taken up, which will lead to a New Revolution- a silent revolution a peaceful revolution.

WHAT WE CAN DO THE OLD WAY OR NEW WAY

When this time of a world trauma comes, and one which most likely is the economy, I assure you there will be other effects as well. Certain countries will begin invading and conquering other lands because the so called moral and free western countries will be busy fighting their own people. It will no doubt be world chaos and a power free-for-all. It can all only lead to more screwed up situations. All of these predators within governments who feed on the people and masses will see others making a power grab, and so based on this will do the same of their own. Why would they not? The timing will be perfect.

So people have got to look at what can be lost here, people have got to look on an individual and collective level. In the end it is always the citizens who are killed, not these crazy leaders who get us into situations like this. There is a lot to be lost here and no doubt world instability and war will be on everyone's mind once that point is reached. At that point in time it will be about leaders fighting other leaders by misusing their people, it will be about different "Mob Families" fighting for control and power, we will simply be collateral damage as far as they are concerned. It will be about their power, what they want, not about people who they could care less about. Look at how they have chosen to prepare for this economy crash as a point. We all have something at stake here.

How does one open people's eyes to the Truth of all of this is the question? "What do we do?", is the other question. We make a choice on a personal level to do something, anything made of positive action and positive energy. This all starts on an individual level. Instead of letting things build to a point of old revolution we change ourselves and put out positive energy.

To begin with each person can start sharing information with others and start speaking out about the injustice and corruption of our times, people can start doing their part to wake others up: it is all about the hundredth monkey effect. Just like corruption, consciousness spreads and grows, consciousness and awareness is the "antibody" and solution to the disease of corruption. So speaking out to others is a good thing to do. Putting out information sheets where others can find them is another- it is simple, positive, and is sure to yield some positive results. We need to make the most of where we are in life for getting the information out, we need to work with what we have. As I get to later, and as an example, politicians need to use where they are in life for doing the same. Work with whatever you have for doing your part for doing good and for doing so constructively.

We need to break this old pattern, this dysfunctional computer program of throwing away our self-empowerment. THAT is the solution and simply by speaking out you have the power to change things. Just as secrecy has the power to change the world (like hiding the existence of aliens) and the future, so does the reversed form of this, speaking out.

There needs to be A War Against Corruption and this needs to be the key focus of each individual, the key focus of the people, this should be everyone's "cause" as this is what is threatening our world and ourselves.. People can not be divided by politics when they are focused on the root problem of our country and world- corruption. This will not only unite people but it will unite people around the correct and proper cause, as the problems of our world are a result of corruption and corrupt people, not various political parties.

Rather than be deterred by the example of WikiLeaks we need to re-double our efforts and support such endeavors. More people need to get involved in similar ways. We need to become aware of the tactics and plans of these corrupt people and we need to speak out about these. We can still change things for the better and we need to work at doing so. By making ourselves familiar with the psychology of this Elite and by making ourselves aware of what they are doing we can change anything. We need to promote consciousness. Consciousness is the way to combat corruption.

Even this economy crash can all be avoided, and if it is avoided the corrupt infrastructure will still have to be removed, these illegal programs exposed and destroyed. No one should be given this power under any circumstances. Neither I, nor my family belong in this as a point, and no one is safe until these programs are exposed. It all needs to be about exposing corruption and bringing goodness back into this world as the dominant flavor and emotion. So far corruption and evil have the upper hand and doing the right thing, being good, is what is illegal and attacked.

Think of your own kids, think of your family, think of your own kind., think of their future and your own. I and my kid have suffered plenty due to corrupt government agents, corrupt programs, and "various things". There is a reason why my first book was titled "Don't Tread On Me". It is a combination of non-thinking non-empowered people and corrupt people, just like in my life, that have made the world into the mess it is and who have made the world into the dangerous place it is.

Speaking from experience, if you are against corruption and against a misuse of power then corrupt people are against you. Your not looking will not change anything, and as a point the agents in my life continue to murder regardless of what people believe. We can not simply ignore things we must do our part. The world this Elite want is not a good world and most people would not agree with the world they want to create, thus they are doing what they can in secret until it will be too late for the masses (that said if the masses were more conscious then things would seem less hidden). These people don't care about the masses, they are so out of touch, megalomaniacal, egotistical, that they have set out to change the entire world in their image. They have decided to change the entire world, so that they can thrive and survive at cost to us.

WE need to change this., WE are the ones who need to be doing something. What we need to do is follow the example of WikiLeaks and Julian Assange, and do our part. We need to put out positive energy for change, and for fighting corruption in whatever way we can. The Truth and power are within us, not outside of us, and this is what people need to realize.

WHAT TO DO: THE PEOPLE AND POLITICIANS ALL WORKING FOR GOOD

So I've spoken here about taking control of one's life, self-empowerment, and speaking out and standing up for what's right. To fight corruption and the deterioration of democracy, which is what corruption is in this case. Both on a personal level and a group level, people have got to work together at this and make it clear that corruption is not acceptable. But what about people in government? People in various intelligence agencies and politicians? What are they doing? Well what I've already stated in the last few pages applies to all people, regardless of one's walk in life. The difference between a sheep and a dog is power and a little bit of knowledge, not blindness.

However the subject of people in governments is a whole different can of worms and the reasons vary. There are good people and evil people in government, for simple terms. Again it gets down to the quality and type of person, not job-title, not a stereotype. That said the ability to change things positively by people within government is all on another level than for most of us, the potential for them to create positive change is even greater.

The corrupt are on the offensive here attacking what is a threat to their power. Good people within government have got to do their part to change this, people within government have got to use their power for good. People within government have got to counter those with power like their own who are corrupt. With good people in government fighting back things will change. Is anyone skeptical that the government is corrupt because of corrupt people? Of course not, so how would government be with enough good people within it doing their part? A lot different I imagine, don't you? People within government need to start promoting goodness and doing the right thing, they need to start holding the corrupt responsible.

When you get to the other side and meet God in whatever form you believe, are you going to say, "I didn't have time for morals and ethics, I was doing my job." Do you honestly believe that this is going to make a lot of sense, does it make any sense now in this life? YOU are responsible for the keeping of your own body and mind, no one else. You are the keeper of your own soul. There are no logical arguments for being weak or passive, for being inactive, for looking the other way.

Good people in government, be it agents or politicians, need to start secretly documenting and releasing information which is what WikiLeaks is about, more people need to start following this example. People in a position to do so need to start exposing corruption and then as more people see this it will turn into a collective movement.

THIS is really what all of this talk about WikiLeaks is about and why they are going after the founder of it-never mind them framing him with rape. It is all about PREVENTING THIS before it can even get started and before it becomes common and acceptable. It is to keep a movement and counter-balancing energy from happening, to silence one before one can start. It is about making a scary example of WikiLeaks to discourage everyone else. No one likes an axe murderer or a rapist, and this is the quickest and easiest way of destroying a good persons reputation as the stigma, accusations, and insinuations alone are enough to distance people. Most have a knee jerk reaction to the accusations without even finding out the Truth, and it does not take anything to accuse somebody of being one. This is all about COINTELPRO and it's smear campaign, it is really all about corrupt politicians, this Elite. That said people within government who are good should be doing their part as well, people within government need to have courage like him and support him. There is an entire country which will support you.

CORRUPTION IS AMERICA'S GREATEST THREAT AND ENEMY AND DESTROYING THE COUNTRY FROM WITHIN: CORRUPTION IS "THE WORLD'S TERRORIST"- anyone disagreeing with this can forget it. Corruption is what people need to be collectively united against. I have had twenty years of corrupt BS and I am absolutely finished with it. I have lost twenty years of my life because of it, and my family has suffered, and still does because of it. I am not a government agent, employee, or politician, but I am doing my part, people within government need to be doing their own. People within government, in terms of Human Physics have more power and concentrated energy than the average person, it is needed that more people within government begin combatting the evil and darkness within government. Again this will encourage all.

As more and more people become self-empowered, active, out-spoken, united, more and more people will become encouraged to do the same. As more people do it, the safer it becomes to do. Just like with corruption, as corruption flourishes more and more people become encouraged to be the same way. So the same principles exist here for doing the right thing, and the more over-burdened the corrupt system becomes at keeping people quiet, the further back corruption is pushed. Self-empowerment and unity spreads from mind-to-mind the way that corruption does except corruption is like a "fatal disease", and self-empowerment is like an "antibody" that empowers the individual and collective. They are flip sides of the same coin, it is all a matter of energy,

Human-Physics. Corruption weakens the collective, self-empowerment strengthens the collective. Again the Elite have to be mirrored, their own techniques and tactics used against them, flipped on them. Obviously the same can be done by government agents, citizens, and politicians.

Most of what is going on these days is illegal and would bring about outrage from the public and the entire country if they only knew. So if you are within government do your part and let the public do the rest. Your end of business is simple. STOP BEING AFRAID ON A PERSONAL LEVEL, THERE IS TOO MUCH AT STAKE. People need to start doing the right thing and fighting for it, these corrupt people belong in prison NOT good people.

Within the next year now, government employees and their families will end up paying just like everyone else. All sorts of people are going to have regrets for going along with the system, and ignoring corruption, when the time comes. The Elite only care about themselves and many within this corrupt system are going to find out the hard way.

By the time you have regrets it will be too late. Contemplate the future. Contemplate the motives of those over you with greater authority, because quite frankly there is nothing great about it. Everyone is looking the other way because there is still another direction to look at, yet very shortly reality will be here, and a lot of people will have regrets. People are looking away out of fear, people are afraid to do their part. Once the future the Elite wants gets here, you will not be able to look the other way: there will only be one direction to look at. Until that time gets here people think there is no harm, or simply want to believe that things will remain fine. This is a matter of wanting to feel comfortable, and being too afraid to speak out, it is a matter of knowing what reality is, but being too afraid to deal with it. This is not good enough anymore, people within government should do their part to protect their country, they should live up to the oaths they have taken and expose corruption as they encounter it. Corruption and corrupt people are the terrorists, not the citizens and people.

POLITICIANS, GOVERNMENT EMPLOYEES, OATHS AND PLEDGES

I have written this as this seems to be a "barrier" for many within government, and an absurd one at that, but I feel it is necessary to address.

In a democracy there should never be secrecy in regards to laws. Secrecy in regards to building military-technologies is one thing (even this is debatable these days), secret-laws in regards to the people is another. Openness is a part of democracy. A government with something to hide is a government to be worried about and one which can not be trusted. Governments hide things from the people because they know they will object- like Stalking and COINTELPRO as a quick example.

But apparently politicians are required at times to sign a pledge of secrecy. For what purpose? Obviously to keep things secret but from who, why, and for what purpose? In this case we have to ask if these secrets are for the betterment of the people or not. That being the case why do they have to be hidden? It already stinks of government doing things which the people are not going to agree to or be happy with, which means that government in these cases is representing itself, not "We the people". Corrupt people represent themselves not others, go figure.

But what is being said? I doubt anything with good intent. We are talking about politicians who are supposedly carrying out the "Will of the people"- there is no need for secrets, unlike the military with it's need to have secrets. Although the military seems to have gone nuts on this point as well, developing and using electromagnetic-technologies against the American people for the purpose of manipulation and control (this one I and my family know). Corrupt politicians are creating illegal laws and the military will enforce these illegal laws, and in doing so betray their country and people. Which is what a dictatorship is about. Both the politicians and military have been infiltrated by these corrupt Elite and their team of henchmen. Obviously I speak of certain individuals, not all, and most of the people in the military are not this way- but when the time comes those going with the flow will be making a mistake. The question is will people in the military defend their people or corrupt politicians when the time comes? But the point is many at the top are filthy and corrupt along with the politicians which is a bad recipe when it comes to the public and masses. With this in mind people within government have got to put aside pledges of secrecy and do their part of speaking out.

So what to do and what about these pledges of confidentiality? Well if lying, manipulations, and deceit are a part of these secret meetings then it needs to be exposed- the American people should not be betrayed. Morals and ethics must come first. Without morals and ethics, without taking personal responsibility, without fulfilling one's oath to one's country first, the country, society, the people, will fall. Preservation of country, people, and self should be motivation enough. People within government doing the right thing, exposing corruption and protecting the people, have an entire country behind them, and that is what you must do: you must start exposing corruption -there is strength in numbers, and politicians need to unite together and start doing this collectively. Good politicians need to unite and start promoting goodness and a War Against Corruption.

Corruption will destroy America, it already is, and so by simple logic we can say that corruption is non-American. CORRUPTION IS AMERICA'S TERRORIST. If it is un-American and within government then it most certainly needs to be exposed. Corrupt politicians are the terrorists, NOT the people. Corrupt politicians are the threat to our country, NOT the people.

What about ones oath to protect the country? Whether you are a politician, in the military, or an agent, if we are willing to die for country, land, and people, then we most certainly should be able to expose corruption for our country, land, and people. And if you are in the military how much sense does it make that you take an oath and pledge to die fighting for your country yet are worried about consequences, jail or even death, in regards to exposing corruption? People have got to do their part, especially since corruption is threatening to destroy America and the world.

America can set itself as a proud example and country again by going after corrupt people, by declaring A War Against Corruption., by setting an example for the world. THAT is what being an American is all about and we will be able to be a proud people again because we are willing to fight for what is right instead of watching the world go to hell while we do nothing. We all have a responsibility here as Americans and as a good people. If we can not fight for goodness, then do we really believe in it? We need to re-find ourselves as individuals and as a country and be a standard bearer for the world again. Simply doing this will re-inspire the world, especially since it is America causing very many of the problems in the first place. We have the ability to do this, it is within each of us. What is inside of us is what counts and what we chose to do is what counts, not a piece of paper, not a pledge of secrecy.

I have been told by the corrupt government agents I'm dealing with, the Clown and her agents, that the Constitution is just a piece of paper with ink and words on it- well so are Pledges of Secrecy. So are illegal laws written with deliberate double meaning so that they can be misused.. The question is when this is the view-point, what should our choice be in regards to such things? The choice should be based on doing the right thing, otherwise how much sense does it make to follow orders on a piece of paper that says to betray your country and your people? It makes no sense, in fact it is a piece of paper that is illegal, never mind the issues involved. Like anyone you are put into a situation of having to do the right thing. Do not remain loyal to criminals who ask you to go along in their criminal enterprises against the country and people, but rather of course expose it. This is not deceit and backstabbing, this is what being an American is about-: having the courage to fight for what is right. As it is you have an entire country willing to stand behind you for exposing what the people need to know and want to know. How hard can it be?

Who says you have to be quiet, scared, and secret? People who in the first place are lying, cheating, and stealing in regards to their country, citizens, agencies, and other politicians. Which is why they have to hide things in the first place. Skip peoples job-titles, we are talking about psychopathic criminals, and powerful organized ones at that. There is no need to be silent in regards to pledges and oaths. YOU DECIDE THAT. Is this your idea of doing the right thing, of being honest, by keeping your mouth shut about other peoples' crimes, lies, manipulations, and deceits? This corruption goes on because the people do not know about it. The corruption goes on because not enough people within government are doing their part to fight corruption.

Too much is at risk. We are all in this together these things affect us all, we all have friends and family. And it is because of a group of negative people doing corrupt tactics and techniques within government that the country is going downhill. America and the world are being deliberately reverse-engineered. More people have got to start caring, and this should be our common bond. Everyone has got to stop thinking that they are alone, and stop being afraid because these criminals are so organized and powerful. They too worry which is why they hide things, and those doing good are not alone, they are never alone. This is about doing the right thing.

Good politicians need to counter-act this corruption with positive energy by secretly releasing inside info about the corrupt plans of these political criminals. Good politicians need to release info about these political criminals and their plans, for the good of all. The actions are the same but the intent is different. ,Good and evil are measured by intentions and in the case of politicians the amount of good they can do, in terms of Human Physics, is even more concentrated. Good politicians doing so will encourage all in a way that few can. The Path of Conscious needs to be chosen by all who prefer consciousness to experience, which in the end will lead to a New Revolution, a peaceful way of change.

NEARING THE END OF THIS CHAPTER AND BOOK

Just like any crime family the Elite are hiring fellow criminals to do their work. As an example, how effective would the Mob be if they hired priests and nuns to do their work? People of similar energy are needed to carry out these jobs and tasks. It couldn't and wouldn't work out otherwise. This is what has happened to government. The corrupt Elite have united bringing in more and more people within government and elsewhere to their side. This is all a battle of evil and good in one very real sense.

More and more corrupt people are being hired, and from experience I can tell you that they are the ones enforcing these illegal government programs. Now it is being passed on to the people, the masses, citizens, society, by secret laws and programs that are allowing COINTELPRO, Mobbing, and fascism to occur. Fascism is a corrupting of one's mind and this is being passed on to the citizens in terms of thinking and actions by government programs, it is a dirtying of the hands of the people- corruption is being passed on and "shared" with the people. By now people ought to realize that fascism is the result of sick minds and is for weak minded people. Psychopaths crave power and the abuse of it, and this is what police states, dictatorships, fascism, are about. My Mobbing speaks of this and it most certainly is not about protecting the people, it is about attacking the people, it is about corrupting the people and getting their hands filthy in regards to another human being. It is all about corruption.

The motto of the Elite is "No good deed goes unpunished", they do not like good people any more than good people like bad people. They are about their own self-interests and will never change. We have got to change instead and change so that we no longer fall victim to their games. It is time for people in large numbers to start choosing the Path of Consciousness. It is time for us to break the mold of our ancestors and history, it is time for a New Revolution.

We all need to unite collectively: citizens, government agents, and politicians. Our common bond needs to be goodness and doing the right thing. This is what these Elite and their team are doing, uniting in corruption and evil. Their own techniques will work against them. By people uniting and pushing back against this corruption it will create an atmosphere of good, and an atmosphere and acceptance of speaking out against corruption. It will become more acceptable to find, seek out, and attack corruption- once this happens a lot of very real powerful criminals can be put away. With functional non-corrupt people in government we will have a functional government that serves the people as it is meant to. The government will become more clean, and no doubt over time the world.

This is not some impossible dream, it is easy to do, people just need to start doing it- and across all walks of life. People have got to begin their own War Against Corruption on a personal level, this is what we all must focus on as corruption and corrupt people are the real "terrorists" here. Corruption is what is threatening our lands, people, and world, not terrorists. Corruption is threatening to destroy us all. People have got to become self-thinking and self-empowered again and choose a new way which will lead to a conscious fixing of our problems without the mess of experience which will result if we do not. It is all simple to see and understand, it is all about energy and people.

More people have got to become self-empowered and do their part. Unify. Find your empowerment and self worth in this world and take action. Simply by doing this we create a greater atmosphere of acceptance for change. Simply by doing this we promote consciousness and change. As corruption spreads from weak mind to weak mind, so does consciousness spread from person to person, the Path of Consciousness grows, and the New Revolution begins. A more intelligent way in which we as a people avoid traumas and conflict, remedying our problems instead through consciousness. Consciousness, the Path of Consciousness and the New Revolution is where it is at and is the only intelligent solution to the problems of our country and world. And it all begins with you.

Dante Kali Das